VATICAN CITY

Valerio Volpini · Tano Citeroni

VATICAN CITY

Art, Architecture, and History

PORTLAND HOUSE
NEW YORK

Edited by Massimo Giacometti
Translated by Cathy Badger

Copyright © 1986 by Motovun (Switzerland)
Copublishing Company Ltd., Lucerne

Copyright © 1986 for the American edition by
Portland House, New York.
This edition published by Portland House,
distributed by Crown Publishers Inc.,
225 Park Avenue South,
New York, New York, 10003.
All rights reserved under International and
Pan-American Copyright Conventions

Lithography by La Cromolito, Milan.
Printed and bound in Yugoslavia.

ISBN 0-517-62280-7

hgfedcba

PICTURE CREDIT
Archives of the Vatican: 151, 192
Belser Publishers, Stuttgart and Zürich: 190, 191
Musei Gallerie Pontificie, Rome: 183
Nippon Television, Tokyo: 188
Scala, Florence: 189
Black & white illustrations: Archive Tano Citeroni

TABLE OF CONTENTS

Mosaic decoration in the drum of St. Peter's dome, executed according to a design created during Pope Sixtus' pontificate by Cavalier d'Arpino.

I – IMPRESSIONS

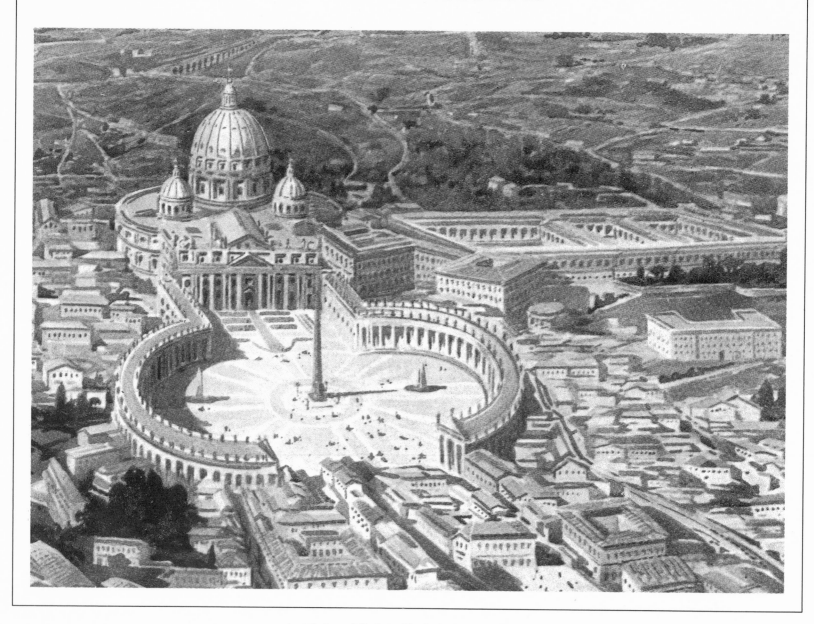

Aerial view of Vatican City before 1930. The design of architects Piacentini and Spaccarelli, which called for the razing of the so-called "Spina di Borgo," dates from 1936. In this photograph, the "Campagna romana" extends right up to the back of St. Peter's, an area which is now completely covered with buildings.

*A*n old saying has it that all roads lead to Rome, and within Rome, all roads lead to St. Peter's Square.

Day after day, from early dawn to the hour when shadows lengthen and the travertine-colored buildings, the sprinklings of green on the hill of the papal University of Propaganda Fide and the white of the statues slowly blend into a uniform gray, Piazza San Pietro is a stage for the entire world. One keen observer has even described the Square as "theater," a literal portrayal of human and holy aspects, in all languages and with all the unique modes of expression to be found on all continents. The "performers" are the visitors, who speak in euphoric, if undecipherable voices that reveal respectful astonishment and heartfelt agreement, and the "natives" of Rome, clearly distinguishable from the cosmopolitan character of the Square, who take part here with much the same matter-of-factness as children who improvise a small soccer match with a clattering soft-drink can as a ball. The "natives" of the Square certainly include the doves, a few sellers of postcards and brightly-colored souvenirs, and an occasional street vendor carrying his portable store around his waist and trying to sell his valuable wares "almost for free."

In every season — even during winter, under a sky either of deep blue or, when the icy west wind is blowing, of shimmering silver — the Square is alive in a way encountered nowhere else. And it belongs to the men, women and children of the entire world: literally everyone feels at home here.

Neither the march of history nor the change nor the succession of cultures has been able to alter this feeling. St. Peter's Square is a meeting-place for all of Christianity, the "reception room" for those who journey here from all corners of the world out of belief or just plain curiosity. The square's atmosphere may vary with the seasons, and its coloring may change with the time of day, but the visitor's strong feeling of being welcome amidst the enclosure formed by the rows of columns and the inviting gestures of the statues remains unchanged.

San Pietro has a life of its own, and only those lucky enough to experience the Square under the most varied conditions can appreciate its uniqueness. In the hours and days not marked by special church activities, when gusts of wind blow scattered scraps of paper into crazy, whirling dances, the Square expresses a playful spirit. Then again, it can appear mysterious when in the evening or night hours it lies deserted, cleft by the maze of barricades set up for the Pope's audiences on Wednesdays, and the stacked chairs resembling bizarre, abstract sculptures.

But there are important events, too. At the church festivals bishops, cardinals, diplomats and invited guests from all walks of life form a corona around the papal altar according to strict rules of ceremony, while the "people" crowd into every available remaining space to the accompaniment of prayers and hymns. At times like these, the Square becomes a temple of Christianity under the city skies of Rome, where the Vatican is a symbol of history — albeit a different history.

The Square is never more beautiful than when seen on the threshold between the usually mild winter and the early Roman spring. Then the subtle tones of the façades, even the paving stones, gain a vivid clarity, almost as if the mild climate also breathed its awakening of hidden and distant nature on the statues and columns. At this time of year the Square is its most impressive at the break of day, when hardly a movement (with the exception of a hurried nun or priest or the handful of uniformed policemen on night duty being relieved of their watch) is to be seen. This is the moment of awakening — neither too hurried, nor too sluggish — and whoever has experienced it is immediately aware that this wide, open space affords a warm welcome to any person appearing then, even if only because he is one of the earliest of the day's expected visitors.

Even if you set off in a straight line for the doors of the basilica, you will find the center of the square difficult to avoid. The harmony of the architectural concept — which is not the product of an artistic whim but the result of Bernini's ingenious creative powers — does not leave the visitor feeling isolated in the broad expanse of the Square, but neither is its solemnity obtrusive, nor does it demand subservience. On the contrary, you can move about unrestrainedly here in the timeless, natural simplicity brought to full bloom in Piazzo San Pietro during the course of its century-long history.

The baroque, expansive gestures of the Square's 164 statues, which evidently maintain direct contact to Heaven and automatically guide our glance upwards, hardly appear to fulfill a function in the compact rows of columns arranged in two half-circles. Yet Bernini's colonnades are full of symbolism, solemnity, power and grace, representing that which is intangible, but nonetheless real, in the feelings of believers. Insofar as it is at all possible for an architect to give expression to theological content, this 17th century artist's arrangement of the Square and its rows of saint's statues under the skies of Rome is at least an attempt to accomplish this feat for posterity.

As soon as the people have disappeared and the rising moon bathes the dome of St. Peter's Basilica an eerie white, the Square reasserts itself, seeming to expand in the dim light and deepening silence. The Square and its surroundings merge so completely that even the noise of the traffic from nearby streets is muted. The obelisk, brought to Rome by Emperor Caligula and set up in the Roman Vatican Circus, towers over the Square. This symbol of an ancient culture and of changing events throughout the millenia suddenly seems to have changed itself: torn from the distant land of the Pharaohs to become witness to violent, terrible contests and games, and then finally moved once again by a bold and memorable feat of engineering, it is now a type of monstrance of the cross, as the inscription in its base reveals.

Do any of the people who either unexpectedly find themselves among Bernini's colonnades on St. Peter's Square, or who are led here by the long and (for Rome) unusually wide Via della Conciliazione, stop to think that they are crossing a border and entering another land? No visible sign indicates this, and nobody asks for a passport of identification. Vatican City receives the world in this Square, not through a barrier at the border, but rather an inviting piazza.

No matter from what direction you approach Rome, Michelangelo's mighty dome (or "er cupolone," as it is called in the dialect spoken in Rome) rises above the astonishingly sharp contours of the sea of roofs when seen from a distance and the hazy gray hills of Rome's surroundings. This dome is Rome, the Vatican, and above all it marks the burial place of St. Peter. No other symbol possesses such scope and expressiveness, for the dome calls forth whole chains of memorable and obscure historical, cultural, religious and political associations.

It may be difficult to imagine, but it can be stated with assurance that there is absolutely nothing that hasn't already been said or written about Rome, especially about the Rome of this basilica and its dome. So why proceed? Because the dome is more than just a symbol. It is a sort of hieroglyph that reveals unique meanings to the visitor experiencing them for himself. It is different from anything the visitor has imagined privately on the basis of countless pictures.

II – EARLY HISTORY

Side view of the basilica and Michelangelo's dome. Engraving by G. B. Falda.

*T*wo thousand years ago, the district in which Vatican City is now located was a remote area between the slopes of Monte Mario, Gianicolo and a loop of the Tiber River. According to Varras, the oracle priests of the Etruscans delivered their prophecies, or vaticini, from the tops of these hills. But according to Aulus Gellius, the name "vatican" comes from the whimpering (vagito, or Latin vagitus) of a baby born here.

The city's origins were inauspicious. Frequently flooded by the rampaging waters of the Tiber, the lower part of its land was always considered unhealthy because it was boggy and infested with mosquitos that have apparently survived throughout the millenia. Even today, no one would deny that this area has the most unpleasant climate in Rome.

Some grapevines were cultivated for wine in the surrounding area, but with miserable results (as the Romans, long wine connoisseurs, discovered to their dissatisfaction). The earth was used to make pottery, but proved ill-suited for this purpose.

And yet the land held value for some. Two infamous Roman emperors, Caligula and Nero, had a circus built on the plain. The circus covered the area now bounded by Piazza Pio XII, Palazzo del S. Ufficio, the Collegio Teutonico and extended from there to the audience hall and on to one side of the basilica's apse. One of its edges was probably located at approximately the place were the left wing of the colonnades starts today. It is thought that a heathen burial ground parallel to the first spur of the hill adjoined what was soon named "Nero's Circus." This, in addition to the spread of the Gospel and the martyrdom of St. Peter, may be the real reason why this area became one of the most highly revered places in the ancient world, surpassed only by Mount Calvary. The area's symbolic value was enhanced by countless Christians who had been condemned to death, martyred in "games" with beasts of prey, crucified or burned alive there.

We mention these particulars, which are still a matter of scientific research, as possible reasons why a small cella (i.e., the chapel of Pope Cletus, built in the first century A.D. and soon to be followed by the Constantinian Basilica) was located in this out of the way, uninviting corner of the world.

Peter of Galilee visited this capital of the ancient world several times and found it a suitable hub for the countless paths necessary to spread the new word of Christ. His last journey ended here around 68 A.D. Christ Himself had sent Peter to Rome and entrusted him with the mission of founding the Holy Church in His name. Tradition has it that, when martyred, Peter "the rock" on which this church was to rest, asked to be crucified head down because he did not deserve to be treated equally with the Lord, even at his execution. Upon Peter's burial, the significance of the blood he shed and his martyrdom were by themselves sufficient to determine the seat of the historical church on earth. This place, the site of the otherwise unremarkable building of Pope Cletus, has always been revered by the faithful as the grave of the first pontiff. It became a consecrated place for Rome's Christian community, to which believers of all possible origins belonged at that time. It also became a place of veneration for those traveling to Rome from afar to visit the grave of the man who had been highly respected by all congregations along the Mediterranean coast.

Of special significance is the fact that so many of Peter's successors to the pontificate were also buried here. The Liber Ponteficalis provides a list of them: Linus, Cletus, Evaristus, Alexander I, Sixtus I, Telesphorus, Hyginus, Pius I and Anicetus and so on, including all popes up to the third century (with the exception of Pope Clement I, who died in exile on the island of Ponza). The list continues until times of persecution, when the graves of the popes were moved elsewhere.

It was during the most fervent phase of the evangelization of Rome that the Emperor Constantine decided to erect a basilica at this consecrated place. It was not until about forty years ago that foundations of smaller structure built around the modest chapel of Pope Cletus (called Anaclet I in the historical records) were discovered. Thus, the heart of the Vatican, the sanctuary, grew up around the bones of a martyr, a practice that would be followed in basilicas and many shrines in Europe thereafter. The first living quarters, lodgings for pilgrims and the domicile of the pope were constructed next to the first basilica.

Constantine legally acknowledged the territorial property of the Church after his military victory in 313 A. D. This act not only granted the Christians complete freedom of religion, it was above all a sign of respect for the Christian faith. In 324, Constantine personally marked the outlines of the enclosing walls and carried twelve baskets of earth to the site in honor of the twelve Apostles as a sign of his humility and reverence. By his actions, Constantine laid the foundations for everything that comprised the secular power of the Church up to a little less than a century ago.

Not much remains of Cletus's first small church or of Constantine's basilica, and even less of the oratories, devotions and prayers that were as much a part of the basilica as its two bell towers, shining mosaics, columns and frescos. But the basilica was considered a masterpiece in its time. Recent excavations have revealed that before the foundations could be laid, a part of Vatican Hill had to be removed and the ancient burial ground and adjacent area filled in. Leveling a necropolis was unheard of at that time in Rome. The only person who could possibly take such a liberty was the emperor himself — and even he had to provide irrefutable and cogent arguments for the proceeding. Apparently, the basilica was meant to be built here, with St. Peter's grave at the center of the shrine, regardless of the area's dreariness and isolation and the difficulties associated with the terrain.

Although the Church's reservations about making certain decrees is well known, Pope Paul VI did not hesitate to declare publicly on the Feast of the Apostle Peter on June 29, 1976: "We are happy to have attained certainty of the truth of what was supposed as early as Pius XII that... the grave of St. Peter is really located here at this venerable place; at exactly the place upon which the awe-inspiring basilica dedicated to the Apostle was erected."

Near the end of the 15th century, Leon Battista Alberti, an architect, officially confirmed the ruinous state of the Constantinian Basilica, which, by that time, had already partially collapsed. Although Pope Nicholas V (1447 – 1455) considered it necessary to replace part of the supporting walls, it was Julius II, a strong-willed pontiff who stirred up a lot of action in his time, who decided to completely rebuild the basilica. With his excellent instinct for the Church's power in secular and especially political matters, and with the ardent zeal of a Renaissance prince, Julius viewed this undertaking chiefly as a chance for the Church to increase its prestige. Moreover, he was fortunate to have at least two generations of first-class artists and several brilliant contemporaries at his disposal.

In April 1506, Julius ordered work on the basilica to be started according to a plan drawn up by Bramante. Less than two years later, the supporting pillars of the new church, designed as a classical Greek cross, had been completed. After the deaths of Nicholas and Bramante, the two fathers of the building, Raphael assumed responsibility for the entire project. His first act was to change the Greek cross, as indicated in the building plan, into a Latin cross. Raphael and his co-workers' concept was followed until the mid-16th century, even after management of construction was entrusted to Antonio Sangallo on the death of the painter from Urbino. Sangallo tried to completely change Bramante's design, but he met with the unyielding resistance of the great Michelangelo, who had recognized the ingeniousness of the design even though he was Bramante's opponent. When Sangallo died, the Pope adamantly insisted that Michelangelo should assume control of the project and design the cupola.

The basilica is considered to have been completed by Michelangelo, except for a competition for the design of the exterior façade opened by Pope Paul V (1606 – 1621) in 1607. Carlo Maderno was awarded the contract and building proceeded according to his plans. Within five years, all remainders of the façade of the original Constantinian Basilica had been torn down. Altogether, work on the basilica had lasted more than a century, from the time of Bramante's labors to the day in November, 1626 when Pope Urban VIII (1623 – 1644) consecrated the mighty work down to its last detail. Indeed, thirteen centuries had passed since construction of the first basilica had begun under Emperor Constantine. The creation of the powerful basilica and its interior and exterior masterpieces of architecture, sculpture and painting span the period of the Renaissance, an era committed to the principles of Classicism, to Mannerism.

III – VATICAN ART AND ARCHITECTURE

Aerial view of St. Peter's, the Gardens, the Belvedere Courtyard, Palazzo Sant'Uffizio, St. Peter's Square and the Spina di Borgo. The latter was razed in 1936 and replaced by Via della Conciliazione.

The piazza, the basilica and the dome form a unique, matchless creation, an "artistic whole", in the sense of the details of its parts and the heterogeneousness of the cultural and historical aspects they reflect. The harmonious framework formed by architecture and sculpture, the overpowering structural proportions, and the mosaics, paintings and other decorations are all integrated and complement each other. The close relationship between all the elements of the basilica seems to allude to the history of the Church and its structure: the workers' great toil has merged with the harmony pursued by the famous artists and the anonymous craftsmen. The spirit of belief manifests itself as the common denominator of this creative will and stands out against one of the most dramatic rents ever to shake the unity of Christianity that also occurred during this century: Martin Luther's Reformation.

Just as one can read great works of poetry again and again, so is the basilica a work of art that even a practiced observer can experience anew, over and over. With a simple change in perspective, it bestows itself upon the visitor as a new gift.

The various parts of the Square show their best sides when viewed from its center. Whoever pauses here can actually feel how the details of the surroundings exert their influence. As if drawn upward by some force, the visitor climbs the stairs to the doors of the basilica – an involuntary, natural reaction to the suggestive power of this magnificent monument to both arcane mystery and reality. The surrealistic play of its elements captures the gaze and enters the mind's eye. It is never superficial, never a mere "object of admiration": this miracle of harmony penetrates deep to become the voice of the spirit.

Facing the five doors one senses the Square left behind as a protective hand on the back. The middle gate, across the atrium, is the work of Filarete. Originally designed for the old basilica, it was only later adapted to the dimensions of the present building. It became the Holy Door, the Porta Sancta, a symbol of the great, all-encompassing compassion of the Lord. It is sealed with a bronze cross and may only be opened by the pope during a holy year, according to a binding regulation for the Catholic church made by Boniface VIII in 1300. The loosely laid brick wall behind the door is easily destroyed by the hammer blows struck by the pope.

Opposite: The Basilica of St. Peter as seen from the fortified walls of Castel S. Angelo, once the Mausoleum of Emperor Hadrian. Pope Alexander VI had a walkway installed in the surrounding wall built by Leo VI (847-855). This walkway, called "Passetto", connected the Vatican Palace with Castel S. Angelo.

St. Peter's Square early in the morning, when few tourists are about. Many famous travelers, including Goethe, Gregorovius and Stendhal, have written about the Square's impressive atmosphere at this time of day.

Opposite: *St. Peter's Square, the Basilica, Vatican Palace and the view of Rome from St. Peter's dome. The torch holders can be seen on Michelangelo's curved dome; up to about fifty years ago, torches were used to light the dome during high ceremonies. Today, the dome and the facade are illuminated electrically.*

Overleaf: *Pope John Paul II amidst a cheering crowd. He was seriously wounded here on May 14, 1981. The Square is now guarded by the Vatican guards during papal audiences and the faithful must pass through barriers erected by the Italian police.*

Nuns enjoying a picnic on Piazza Pio XII in front of Bernini's elliptical square. Obtaining food and drink is a problem for the faithful on Sundays. Many rest under the colonades and eat what they have brought with them or bought on the previous day. A hustle and bustle dominates St. Peter's

Square, especially around the fountains. The time of the midday prayers, with its banners honoring the pope, colorful balloons, people in their native costumes, singing, dancing, prayers and choir music, is particularly appealing.

Opposite: *The statue of St. Paul on the right-hand side of the Square was created by Adamo Tadolini and set up before 1840. Because it seldom snows in Rome, this view of St. Peter's Square covered with snow is rare.*

Overleaf: *Maderno's fountain. In the early morning hours, the doves that nest under Bernini's colonnades take their baths here. Especially on warm summer evenings when the fresh breeze called "venticello" blows, St. Peter's Square entices the visitor to take a walk.*

St. Peter's Square is a meeting place for faithful and clergy from throughout the world.

Above right: *The fountain with the four tiaras was made in the first half of the 20th century. In the background you can see the right-hand semicircle of Bernini's colonnades and, behind that, the Apostolic Palace and Borgia Tower.*

Opposite: *The statue of St. Peter seen from Braccio di Carlomagno (the section of the colonnades named for Charlemagne). The Swiss Guard is wearing a full-dress uniform with white gloves and halberd.*

First overleaf: *Two bishops on their way to a ceremony in the Vatican. The colonnades are comprised of 284 columns and 88 pillars and are decorated with 140 statues of saints and martyrs, as well as large coats of arms from Pope Alexander VII.*

Second overleaf: *View of St. Peter's Square, with the 41-meter-tall obelisk from Heliopolis in its center. The Square can accommodate up to 200,000 people.*

No matter if they sell reproductions of St. Peter's or statues in the Vatican Museums, tapestries with the picture of John Paul II, or postcards and posters; the souvenir business flourishes. In Via del Maschinero, not far from the door of St. Anne, there is even a supermarket for religious objects.

Above top: *The statue of St. Peter towers over the stacks of chairs for the general audiences on Wednesdays.*

Upon entering the basilica, visitors usually first become aware of how greatly their impression of its dimension's differs from its actual size. The two putti underneath the shell-shaped holy water font, for example, at first appear dainty, only upon standing to them does one realize just how gigantic they really are. Yet it is not so much the grandeur that enthralls, but the general naturalness of proportion, which Luca Pacioli called "divine" in his theoretical treatise written around the turn of the 16th century.

Tourist guides, who tend to take a bookkeeper's attitude towards their job try to capture the magnificence of this building in numbers: in hundreds of marble, bronze and travertine columns as well as in hundreds upon hundreds of statues made of the same materials and of plaster. These figures have been inscribed on the floor of the central nave, together with information about the lengths of other important European cathedrals and basilicas. But every one of these works calls for more than just a fleeting glance while passing by. One visit to the basilica demands another, then another, and yet another... The discovery and contemplation of a particular detail inevitably leads to the next detail. History and faith; art and culture; knowledge and tradition; church history and the history of the world; the finitude of worldly power and spiritual immortality − all of these blend together, alternate and superimpose themselves in such a manner that almost every visitor is compelled to focus on particular segments, thus gaining an effective if extremely simplified overall view.

Neither the most minor of artistic schools nor a single form of expression in occidental art from the Renaissance to the present are missing in the labyrinthine, repeatedly altered rooms of the basilica. If the other works of art stored especially in the grottos − which comprise a sort of "underground basilica" − are also included, it can even be said that two thousand years of the history of European art are collected here.

This amassed splendor may irritate the religious sensitivities of some, but we should not forget that the wealth and honor of this highest temple in Christianity had an extremely bitter reverse side. The secular component of Ecclesia carrying the entire load of its ties to the events of the times − a load which increased over the centuries and with the sins and weaknesses of the people involved − is a part of the church that cannot be neglected.

But the absolute perfection of the elements comprising the wealth of the basilica mirrors the beliefs of many generations. The creative force of inspiration was given wings by religious stimulation. Whoever views the Pietà created by the young Michelangelo is also influenced by the great power of this internal tension. A deep spirituality and faith have been embodied in the Pietà. Michelangelo was not yet twenty-four when he heard that some uninformed admirers had attributed his Pietà to another artist. Only then, according to the story, did he insist upon adding the inscription "Michael Angelus Bonarotus florent. faciebat" ("Michelangelo Buonarotti from Florence created this").

When walking down the right-hand side of the church, each chapel along the way provides a reason to pause for a detail, or an ensemble, or merely because of the skilled craftsmanship evident in a decoration. You could pause, for example, in the Capella del Sacramento because of its overpowering, gleaming abundance of baroque elements or the precious arabesques in the delicate ironwork of the gate.

It may seem odd that monuments to three "secular" women are located amongst all the statues of founders of religious orders and popes, the portrayals of biblical figures and the various memorials in the basilica, and that relics of two of them are kept. These three women – Princess Mathilda of Canossa, Marie-Christiene of Sweden and the daughter of a Polish prince, Maria Clementina Sobieski – represent chapters of church and papal history in its entangelement with all the reservations and prejudices of the contemporaries who helped write this history. However, it must be admitted that such reservations never exerted a controlling influence; on the contrary, they were always subordinate to the higher truth and mystery towards which the Church is oriented. What today may seem to be an anachronism or even an erroneous path followed by the Church has to be seen in light of the values and cultural conditions of the different epochs. This huge basilica is thus also a sort of history book and a witness to some highly dramatic historical events.

The heart of the basilica, the tomb of St. Peter, is located directly under the highest point of the dome. The high altar (confessio) above the resting-place of the martyr, was erected here and covered by Bernini's dark gold canopy. Seventy oil lamps glow faintly here as a sign of devotion. You can descent two short flights of stairs from here to the semi-circular crypts below.

Pope Innocent III (1198 – 1216) in a mosaic from the apse of old St. Peter's Basilica. In the "Museo di Roma."

The four spiral columns of bronze that support the canopy are masterpieces of baroque art. In spite of their massiveness, the supporting shafts appear light and lively in a way typical of the 17th century. Bernini was ordered to procure the bronze he needed for the columns from the Pantheon (bronze having gradually become scarce as a result of the rapid developments in cannon building). That pope responsible for this "plundering" came from the Barberini family, which is proved beyond a doubt by the honeycomb pattern contained in his coat of arms. The citizens of Rome, who had already suffered through the sack of Rome by the barbarians, made up the saying at that time, "Quod non fecerunt barbari, fecerunt Barberini": "Whatever the barbarians spared, the Barberini took." (Actually, the monuments of ancient Rome had been serving as stone quarries and sources of other building materials for centuries.)

The glittering globe of the dome, with its decorative mosaic friezes, rises above the elegant, upwardly spiraling monumental canopy. At the foot of the dome's drum, appropriately, is the solemn saying for the founding of the Holy Church for the faithful: "Tu es Petrus et super hance petram aedificabo Ecclesiam meam". ("You are Peter and upon this rock I will build My church.") The cathedral (chair) located in the apse behind the high altar, like the canopy above the altar of the confessio, is another monument created by Bernini to glorify the prince of apostles. He built a mighty reliquary around the chair, supposed at the time to be that of the first Apostle. The chair in question though, a wooden structure decorated with ivory, is now known to have been brought to Rome by Emperor Charles the Bald for his coronation and then given to the pope.

The Holy Ghost itself seems to illuminate the angel-surrounded throne. The throne is the symbol of the triumphant threefold power, of the threefold crown (tiara) which is touched — indeed, all but supported — by four scholars of the church to indicate that the authority of the Holy See would not exist without the bishops and that, in turn, the authority of the bishops would be unthinkable without that of the pope. Not only infallibility, but also the principle of community spirit, are already suggested in Bernini's work. It is as rich in precious materials (marble, bronze, gold and glass) as it is in allegories, which were quite obviously dictated to the artist by Catholic theologians according to the strict orthodoxy of the Counter Reformation. Each surrounding detail, each unfilled space and the light falling from the heights of the dome together seem to guide the eyes of the visitor to one fixed point in the area where the confessio stands: the altar.

There is a fitting saying in the Roman dialect for jobs that never seem to be completed: ". . . like in the factory (building hut) of St. Peter's Basilica." This is a reminder that the basilica is not a museum, even if it does seem so to many visitors. People who merely cling to their guidebooks may, indeed, leave with the superficial impression of absolutely perfect works of art, but they will have no idea of the spirit that stands behind the poetry. You have to have experienced St. Peter's basilica yourself, during the papal ceremonies on occasion of the high feasts of the Catholic church year, when the pontiff celebrates mass at the altar of the confessio, surrounded by cardinals in red and bishops in purple, by priests, guests of honor and believers whose hymns echo in the vaults. The basilica embraces a solemn, festive and joyful crowd of people and pilgrims from all corners of the world during these Christian festivals and in such moments, the highest temple of Christianity becomes catholic in the original sense of the word: universal and all-encompassing. No matter if it is a church ceremony, a rite of beatification, the consecration of a bishop, or any other occasion — the basilica unfolds its true beauty only during the performance of the rites. Each element, whether antique or very new, becomes a part of the spiritual communion.

There is not much left of the Constantinian basilica, Old St. Peter's, but as though to strengthen the continuity between the two churches, the few existing remains are contained in the grottos. In addition, the bronze statue of St. Peter, attributed to Arnolfo di Cambio, was certainly created before 1300. Furthermore, one tomb was left here, the grave of Innocent VIII (the last one of the many that were located here at one time) across from the spacious chancel in which the canons gather to recite psalms.

"The Original Sin," one of Raphael's frescos in
the loggias.

IV – THE RENAISSANCE
AND THE FOUNDING OF THE VATICAN STATE

The pedestal of the memorial column by Antonino Pio (138 – 161 A.D.), restored under Pope Leo XIII. In the "Musei Vaticani," Rome.

About three meters below the many-colored floor of the basilica is a second church that was created as a result of the gap between the floor of the present church and the floor of the Constantinian basilica. This space was opened up under the name of "grotte vaticane" during the first half of the twentieth century. A "suberranean church," it stretches from the point under the confessio altar to approximately the middle of the central nave. Some 147 popes are buried here, including several who left lasting marks on the history and art of Europe: Leo the Great, who confronted the Huns/Gregory the Great, for whom the Gregorian chant and a liturgical rite were named; and Sixtus IV, who commissioned the Sistine Chapel. Popes of more recent times include St. Pius (Pius X), and Pius XI, who ended the strife between the papacy and the Italian government and became the founder of the State of Vatican City by act of the treaties of 1929. In addition there are the tombs of Pius XII, the "protector of Rome"; John XXIII, who convened the Second Vatican Council; and finally the tomb of Paul VI, the pope who renewed the post-council church and prepared it for the transition into the third millenium.

The veneration for the tombs and the dim light in the crypts create a secretive, mysterious atmosphere. The insignia of ancient piety were set up next to the national chapels, which were only opened a few decades ago. In these chapels, where pilgrims can celebrate the rites in their native tongues, yet always remain conscious of the fact that they are also standing at the grave of St. Peter — an association between belief and commemoration that has existed at this spot for almost two thousand years. Whoever descends into the crypts after spending some time in the vast basilica cannot escape a curious influence: suddenly, it is unexpectedly easy, almost "natural," to be innerly serene and to commune with the past. At a depth of approximately seven meters, measured from the level of the present-day basilica, parts of a Roman necropolis were uncovered during the last excavations. The investigations led Pius XII to instigate a search for concrete evidence to confirm what tradition had always said about Peter's grave. This archeological undertaking has a significance for Christianity that transcends its purely cultural-historical aspect. An encounter with the Greek inscription "Petrus eni" ("here is Peter") — with the remains of the first small church and Constantine's mausoleum, the altars that lie around it and the dome high above, flooded with light and bearing a cross on top — has a spiritual context that points to the life after death.

The elevator only ascends as high as the roof of the basilica. The visitor who moves around between small domes on the traversable roof will be astonished again and again with new, unexpected views. The structures on the roof could be a small village clinging to the side of a mountain: the dome dominates everything. If you want to climb it, though, you have to go the rest of the way on foot.

You visitor now stands at the upper edge of the façade, at the foot of the row of statues, and here for the first time he becomes aware of their real dimensions. The city panorama appears distant and blurred, but the surrounding mountains, blue or green according to the light, are delineated sharply against the horizon. The noise from the traffic below can hardly be heard up here, and already you start to feel a bit removed from the present, conveyed into a limbo between antiquity and unreality. Were it not for the faces and voices of the people around you, you would feel as though you had been transported into a metaphysical painting. Standing on the rooftop of the basilica is like standing on a little island of the soul.

Michelangelo felt that his work on the cupola was the supreme expression of his creative spirit. It was certainly his most difficult task. Yet for Michelangelo, the work meant more: it challenged all his pride and ambition. It was not "merely" a matter of imagination and inventiveness, but also a conscious attempt to exceed the limits of technical possibilities in his time. First and foremost, this was an adventure that demanded fulfillment. From the very beginning, Michelangelo had planned a spherical shape for the dome, yet at the same time added the reservation, "Practice will teach us during construction just how much we will really be able to accomplish." Michelangelo risked everything for this project, including everything he had already accomplished as a sculptor and painter. He asked neither wages nor a reward, but plunged into the work out of sheer love for the basilica. Pope Paul II gave witness to this when he stated "Nullo praemio, nullave mercede" ("No reward, no pay at all").

The project was realized in part with the help of those who had initially turned the other way. The work of the great artist from Florence, which depended so heavily on the art of bricklaying and on the experience gained in daily practice, was in no way betrayed by their indifference. It is possible that Michelangelo had even anticipated with the disapproving reactions of his contemporaries. At any rate, the dome was completed in less than two years. Eight hundred workers toiled day and night on the cupola for twenty-two months (much to the satisfaction of the lighting crew who, according to the reports of the chroniclers, were able to put in quite a bit of overtime). After July 15, 1588, the day when Sixtus V (1585 – 1590) appproved the building commission – an unusually strong-willed pope and a reformer of the Curia and the state – even opponents of the project began to change their opinions. On May 15, 1590, the last stone was laid over the inner aperture of the dome. The event was "celebrated with great exuberance and thundering of the artillery". Vasari, an art critic and architect, praised the entire project enthusiastically in his report, and gave eloquent testimony about it as an expert and contemporary. "It (the dome) is of such ingenious and well-considered construction and of such excellent craftsmanship that no one, not even an expert, can ever before have seen a more graceful, more beautiful and more artistic work; not only in regard to the bonds and joints of the masonry, but also in respect to the fact that secular power and eternity have been joined in this edifice..."

If you stand inside the basilica next to the altar of the confessio and look upwards, the dome appears ponderous, even threatening. The light of its lanterns seems to flood down as through an opening in dark clouds. Yet if you gaze down into the dizzying depths of the cupola from above, you will hardly be able to believe how tiny Bernini's mighty canopy suddenly appears as dainty as a knick-knack on a chest of drawers. From up above, you also become aware of the compactness of Vatican City. If you threw a coin, it would land on the other side of the state border, in Italian territory. It is true that in one direction, at least, the border is not as distant as the dome is high. Like a brightly colored cadastral map, this tiny state and its integral components spread out below the beholder: the basilica in the piazza, the Vatican buildings and the Vatican Gardens. Just as the monastery and cloister should be located next to the monastery-church and the pastor's residence next to the church, so the Apostolic Palace, the Vatican Palace, rises next to St. Peter's. It is more accurate, though, to speak in the plural, of palaces, since we are referring to a many-sided complex of buildings that has arisen and been repeatedly altered and enriched throughout its history.

When viewed from Piazza San Pietro, Bramante's three-part loggias stand out against the Court of San Damaso (Cortile S. Damaso), as does the Sistine Chapel located a bit further in the background. Originally, the papal residence was the heart of this ensemble of buildings, which has expanded from pontificate to pontificate and century to century and thus bears traces of all different styles and schools of architecture. However, the popes only used the residence occasionally, because the actual seat of the Bishop of Rome is located in the Lateran Palace next to the Basilica of S. Giovanni. For centuries, the Basilica S. Pietro was situated "abroad," in an outlying area clearly separated from the City.

Possibly because of a schism that had divided the Roman congregation, Pope Symmachus had to take refuge in the building erected next to the basilica towards the end of the fifth century. He remained there for five years, during which time he had additional living quarters built, the so-called "episcopia" (bishops' apartments). These were enlarged and decoarted by his successors.

Charlemagne had an existing building enlarged into an imperial residence, whereas Pope Leo IV (847 – 855) ordered a fortified wall to be erected around the territory of the Vatican. What little remains of this wall still bears his name. Even at that time, this circular wall already indicated the extent of the future Vatican City – autonomous, fortified and clearly separated from the city of Rome, to which it actually belonged. Thus arose the first Vatican City.

The wall was built because the basilica had to be protected from both the pillaging of invaders from the North and the raids of the Saracenic pirates, who approached Rome from the mouth of the River Tiber. Subsequent popes also reinforced the defensive works and the buildings inside the enclosure. Nicholas III (1277 – 1280) was especially noteworthy in this respect. Ferdinand Gregorovius, the famous German cultlural historian of the nineteenth century, reports that Nicholas III had a number of new buildings erected and was particularly concerned with strengthening the fortifications of the enclosures surrounding the gardens. A quarter century after completion of the work commissioned by Nicholas III the first conclave was held in the Vatican, at which Benedict XI (1303 – 1304) was elected.

The new buildings, including the residence of Pope Nicholas, were all located on the Vatican Hill side of Vatican City. They are now incorporated into the Cortile del Pappagallo, which represents the oldest existing part of the Apostolic Palace. According to recent technical investigations, some remains are still to be found. However, most of the old structures were destroyed to make room for the new buildings of the Renaissance. It should be called to mind that not until Gregory XI (1370–1378) did the popes return to Vatican City to take up residence permanently, after nearly seventy years of dwelling in Avignon. No one is certain if this decision was made deliberately or was due only to the fact that the Lateran Palace had been destroyed by fire.

Although a part of the "palatium novum," the so-called "New Palace" of Nicholas III is a relic of the Middle Ages and thus the oldest of all buildings still in existence. The completion of the palazzo nuovo closed an important chapter of building activity and city-planning in the Vatican that had been concentrated in the area around Peter's grave and the Constantinian basilica. The little that still stands today can hardly be identified anymore as a part of the original palace.

For longer than two hundred years, from the end of the 15th century until well into the 17th century, constant expansion and change dominated the scene. Almost all succeeding popes left their marks on architectural development of the city. During the Golden Age of Humanism and the Renaissance, every significant Italian city adorned itself with public and private palaces, from Florence to Ferrara, Milan to Urbino and Naples to Venice and Mantua. Of course, these palaces would not have been complete without masterpieces of sculpture and painting. Virtually every city ruler and prince became the patron of the transformation of his city, thereby laying the groundwork for changes in daily life, too, in accordance with the Renaissance cult of beauty and elegance. The rulers of the city-states competed against one another, emphasizing their political standing and power through showing off and one-upmanship in cultural achievements.

It is no wonder that the popes of that period also felt deep ties to the spirit of the Renaissance. Indeed, because they were conscious of ruling over more than just a worldly empire, they considered themselves to belong to a higher rank. In addition, they lived in a society which placed special importance on cultural values and as a rule were themselves well-educated and highly learned men. This is particularly true of Nicholas V (Tommaso Barentucelli, 1447–1455), Pius II (Enea Silveo Piccolomini, 1458–1464), Paul II (Pietro Barbo, 1464–1471) and Sixtus IV (Francesco della

Rovere, 1471 – 1484). The principles of the "cause" they served and their spiritual power were not thought to contradict the cultivation of art and beauty at all — on the contrary, in awareness of their rule not being limited to the secular world they often took the cult too far. This exubernt desire to create art is first to be noticed in Nicholas V, who initiated the construction of the palace. A certain Rucellai from Florence, who made a pilgrimage to Rome in the Holy Year of 1450, described the building as something "extraordinary" (and someone who came from Florence was neither ignorant nor easily impressed).

A collection of approximately 800 codices kept on the second floor of the palace forms the nucleus of one of the most unusual collections in the world, the Vatican Library, which was to earn an unparalleled reputation thanks to the determined support of Sixtus IV. This was the same pope who had the chapel now known as the Sistine Chapel built next to the library. Sixtus's successor, Pope Innocent VIII (1484 – 1492) ordered the ground north of the chapel broken for construction of the Belvedere Palace, which in the course of time merged and became one with the existing complex. For over half a century, from Nicholas to Leo X (Giovanni Medici, 1513 – 1521), the Vatican more or less remained a construction site. For this reason, it also became a focus of unusual cultural activity, a meeting place for the great artists of those times who, each in his own way, left behind evidence of his genius. This epoch — which encompasses the creation of the Sistine Chapel, the loggias, the Palace of the Borgias and the suites of apartments (stanzas) decorated in the names of Julius II and Leo X — is comparable only to the era of Pericles in Athens or of Emperor Augustus. A second generation of first-class artists began to emerge while the first generation, which included such artists as Botticelli, Ghirlandaio, Andrea del Castagno, Fra Angelico and Piero della Francesca, was still active. This is also the age of the strongest secularization of the Church, when raison d'état either completely supplanted the substance and religious mission of the Church or at least relegated them to a minor position. This is the time when, for example, Alexander VI (Rodrigo de Borgia, 1492 – 1503) not only had his private chambers decorated with frescos by Pinturicchio, but also had his own family's emblem, the bull of Valencia, inscribed there. During this era, several pontiffs had the Church serving them more than they served it.

Benvenuto Cellini showing Pope Paul III (1534 – 1549), the first Roman pope after a period of 103 years, a censer. The print is a more popular one from the mid-19th century.

Pope Julius II (Giuliano della Rovere, 1503–1513) had no desire to remain any longer than necessary in the chambers of his predecessor (and rival). Whether or not he also wanted to clearly mark a turning point, he had the ostentatious quarters remade into three much more modest rooms and added a fourth, which was quite a bit more spacious. Although Piero della Francesca and Luca Signorelli had already immortalized themselves in work on the chambers and Sodoma and Perugino were still at work, this irrepressible, strong-willed pontiff, who had known Raphael as a twenty-five-year-old, ordered all existing chambers torn down and entrusted Raphael with the management of the entire project. Raphael worked here from 1508 until his death in 1520. The stanzas decorated by Raphael did indeed become one of the highlights of the art of painting and a testament to human genius. Among other things, they portrayed the decisive cornerstones in the history of the Church, especially the dogmatic and theological aspects of important Church principles. Raphael's combination of religion and culture produced results that have given evidence of his unusual creative powers down through the centuries.

The pope's expertise and sagacity (today we would call it "critical awareness") were so exclusively oriented towards Raphael's genius that, for Raphael's sake Julius had some earlier adornments created by other great artists destroyed. Julius persuaded a resistant Michelangelo to enlarge and add on to his painting according to the pope's own wishes. Although Michelangelo protested and claimed he was really a sculptor, Julius insisted that Michelangelo obey his command, with results that an unusually well-read and knowledgeable Vatican art historian describes as follows. "The playful, almost festive self-assuredness of Raphael confronts the dramatic taciturnity of Michelangelo in the vault of the Sistine Chapel. It is true that Raphael's song unfolds into the almost unattainable counterpoint in respectful observance of all the rules of harmony, however, it is not allowed to dissolve into unity; in other words, the song fulfills neither its stated intent nor a melodic transcendency, both once part of its original potential. Whereas he did open up new spatial effects for the art of painting, at the same time the expansive gestures and an agile, powerful discourse escape this truly great master. Even before he (Michelangelo) expresses them, he mutes them in his superior, man-of-the-world style. Michelangelo is an obstinate hermit well able to do without song and discourse. He tends more to silence – but when he does open his mouth, he roars." (Ennio Francia: La città del Vaticano, Rome, 1947.)

For a very long time, thousands upon thousands of men and women from throughout the world have filed past these masterpieces every season of the year. These works of art are monuments to the human mind that no one can ignore. Goethe once said something to the effect that whoever had not seen the Sistine Chapel could not comprehend the extent of man's capabilities. Famous remarks such as this also are a part of church history. They refer positively to secularization, to the bright side of the church's "worldliness."

Neither Raphael nor Michelangelo confined themselves to the above-named works. As already mentioned, Raphael assumed management of the entire project after Bramante's death (1514) and decorated the second loggia himself. He left the rest to a trusted staff of coworkers. At the sovereign insistence of two popes, Clement VII and Paul III, Michelangelo also finally agreed to paint the front wall of the Sistine Chapel, the other walls already having been covered with frescos by outstanding artists. Finally, Paul III had a private chapel built for the express purpose of creating further wall space for Michelangelo's frescos.

Today, the cardinals gather in the Sistine Chapel for the conclaves at which new popes are elected. They make their choice in the presence of these dramatic pictures and the man chosen directs his first words as pope to the world from this room – words that as a rule indicate the program of his pontificate.

There is an intimate connection between art and faith here that is only perceived after frequent visits to this place and its works of art; that is, on the condition that you let the intimacy and secrecy, at times even the terribleness, touch you by accepting unreservedly the changing human and historical norms. This does not necessarily require penetration to the depths of a truth that cannot be measured according to the criteria of reason so much as to one that encompasses the mystery of redemption and salvation. The Church stands for this salvation in the name of Christ, whose representative on earth the pope is (at least for Catholics).

When seen from Piazza S. Pietro, the basilica and the palaces occasionally appear to be other-worldly in their natural architectural harmony and their overpowering "rightness." They do indeed form their own world in which the echos of the past have died away and the noisy hustle and bustle of the present has no chance of penetrating. Even the stroke of the hour chimed by the clock on the basilica seems to linger enigmatically. The singular impression made by the truly gigantic basilica is muted and mitigated by the aesthetic counterbalance of the symmetric palazzi. From whatever location the ensemble is viewed, the overall impression of harmony is never lost. Old and new, a medieval fragment and a classical statue, the sarcophagus with heathen symbols and another with Christian ones, a relic of the ancient Constantinian basilica, a decorated stone block of uncertain origin, the ornaments added to the doors by a contemporary sculptor, and the balcony built above the pope's private chambers allowing the guard a few steps in the fresh air — these are all motifs that blend timelessness with an unusual liveliness and that relate to each other so intimately that all abstraction and breathtaking unreality appear eloquently animated. If all this can be traced back along a chain of causes, as it were, to the mortal remains lying in one single grave, then it is only fitting that this should be the house of the living pope, the pope who steps out onto the loggia of the basilica after his election to the apostolic succession to pronounce the benediction of the city and the world (urbis et orbis) and who appears every Sunday at a window of the top story to bless pilgrims and believers after a short talk. The ancient harmony of time and the steadfast stability of tradition — both, in their way, symbols of an unshakable self-assurance — are brought to life by the presence of the shepherd. He is the means and the end of an institution unequaled in the entire world, even if this institution resembles other forms of government in many respects and perhaps also has to deal with the same concrete problems as they do. This government claims to be fundamentally different from all others in its origin as well as in its goals, a difference that has been preserved throughout the centuries and that has determined the weal and the woe of this rule for an equal period of time.

Opposite: *The dome of St. Peter's, designed by Michelangelo, is 132.5 meters high. It was built by Giacomo della Porta with a few minor alterations during the pontificate of Pope Sixtus V (1585-1590). The 140 statues of saints were made by pupils of Gian Lorenzo Bernini.*

The statue of St. Paul at the foot of the stairs to the Basilica. In the background are two statues of saints on the balustrade. A true story has it that, during a conclave, a Swiss photographer took a picture of the sheet of numbers held in St. Paul's hand. He bet on those numbers in the lottery and won a considerable sum of money.

Left: Statues on the left-hand side of the colonnades, seen early in the morning on Palm Sunday. This picture was taken from the roof of "Braccio di Carlomagno".

During the early morning hours, St. Peter's Square is closed to traffic. Since the attack on Pope John Paul II in 1981, only a car from the Italian police cars stand guard during the night.

Right: *One of the 140 travertine statues on the balustrade. Caligula brought the obelisk from Heliopolis to Rome in 37 AD as a decoration for the circus later named for Nero. In the Middle Ages, it was believed that Caesar's ashes were kept in a golden urn in the top of the obelisk. Today, a relic of the Holy Cross is contained there.*

The view from Maderno's fountain to the slopes of Gianicolo and the Romanesque bell tower of San Lorenzo in Piscibus. It is also called San Lorenzino due to its small size.

Left: *View of St. Peter's Square with the Apostolic Palace, Raphael's loggias, Maderno's foundain and Michelangelo's dome.*

Overleaf: *Carlo Maderno's facade, built between 1607 and 1614 for Paolo Borghese, being decorated for one of the great festivals.*

The Holy Father recites the "Angelus" prayer and bestows the Sunday blessing from the window of his study in the Apostolic Palace built during the pontificate of Pope Nicholas V. Pope John Paul II works in this room until about 10:30 p.m., when the lights are extinguished. Sometimes, groups of believers request the pope to come to the window with loud cries, but he has only complied once, at the beginning of his pontificate, when about 20,000 people clamored for his appearance.

Right: *Believers - Catholics and non-Catholics - come from throughout the world to the papal audiences on Wednesdays. Here, a group of nuns prays while Pope John Paul II bestows his first Sunday benediction in 1978.*

On Easter Sunday, John Paul II pronounces the "urbi et orbi" benediction of the city and the world from the Loggia delle Benedizioni (on Maderno's facade). This ceremony is broadcast worldwide every year.

The columns of the church and the entire square are gaily decorated. A cross precedes the Holy Father during the procession.

The Swiss Guard was established in 1506. It is said that Michelangelo designed their full-dress uniform.

According to the Lateran Treaty ("concordate") of February 11, 1929, Italy recognizes the Città del Vaticano as an independent state. The city has its own stamps, its own postal service and its own coins (also circulated in the Italian republic) and runs its own radio station. Its train station connects to the Italian railroad network.

Opposite: A huge crowd on St. Peter's Square during a festival. The statue of St. Paul was erected before 1840 to replace the statue of Peter carved by Paolo Taccone between 1461 and 1462 and now located in the seat of the former Museo Patriano.

The cups for the ceremony of the Eucharist are in place in front of St. Peter's Basilica in the Square. Approximately 100 priests administer the rite of Holy Communion to the faithful.

Right: Many clergymen are needed to ensure that all believers can receive Holy Communion.

On top: *The general audience with the pope takes place in St. Peter's Square every Wednesday. Numerous laborers set up the papal platform and the rows of chairs the night before.*

Above: *The Holy Father performs a papal ceremony in the forecourt of the church during a rite of canonization.*

Opposite: *The Holy Door, which is opened by the pope for jubilees, is made of bronze leaves divided into six sections. A part of the old Basilica, it was built by Antonio Averulino (called Filarete) on commission of Pope Eugene IV between 1433 and 1435. Pope Bonifacius VIII opened the first holy year on February 22, 1300. Jubilees were first celebrated every 50 years, then every 33 years, and finally every 25 years. The opening of the Holy Door on December 24 is also conducted in three other patriarchal basilicas: Sao Paolo Outside the Walls, Santa Maria Maggiore and San Giovanni of the Lateran.*

A section of Maderno's portico adjacent to the Scala Regia. In the background a part of the Apostolic Palace, which was built by Martino Ferralano and Giovanni Vasanzio under the direction of Maderno.

Remembrance and spiritualization of the full weight of history means that the tragedies and severe trials within the church, just like its scandals, must not be suppressed or made light of for they are indicative of the Church's respective holiness and misery. Although this institution was founded by Christ, it was entrusted to human guidance from the very beginning and as a "work of man," it has always swung between the poles of holiness and sinfulness. What were the fates of the men who lived in these palaces, wandered down these halls and paused in front of the same paintings that we stop at even today? These men lived for the Church and at the same time not rarely for the dramatic intoxication of power. Their personal histories flow into the history of the Church, its spirit, its tolerance, its empathy and its beauty. Even during the most turbulent and striking moments that the Church wielded secular power when the popes (like other monarchs) had to make political and military decisions, they always remained aware of the characteristic difference and superiority of their raison d'être and their religious task. This is indeed a long history that reflects cultures, traditions and customs in all their respective peculiarities. Worldly power, which today is considered to be a burden and a restriction on the religious character of the Church, undoubtably slowed and hampered their progress. Nevertheless, it was not able to deform the essence of a spiritual, religious truth that it is the Church's duty to protect.

To the visitor looking out from the top of the dome to the borders and landmarks of this small state, the monument to nearly twenty centuries of history hardly appears any larger than the small park he can see off in the distance in Rome. The burial places, expecially the grave of St. Peter, deep in the grottos, bear breater witness to dramatic upheavals. Centuries of faith and unbelieving, of power and fame, of human passions and human saintliness, are compressed into Vatican history — even though the present "state of Vatican City" is only half a century old.

The Constantinian edict granted not only freedom of religion, but also full legal standing and legitimate ownership of landholdings, property and estates, even those not reserved exclusively for church purposes. Within one century of the edict's proclamation the property of the Church had increased considerably as a result of donations and, during the late Middle Ages, the addition of hermitages and cloisters. In view of the political decline and internal conflicts amongst the quar-

Opposite: *The Basilica of St. Peter and the columns in the entrance under the Loggia delle Benedizioni are decked in splendid array for the Feast of St. Peter and St. Paul on June 30. The pope performs a choral mass in the Basilica, and the musical direction is usually entrusted to an internationally known person. In 1985, Herbert von Karajan was invited to direct.*

Opening of the Holy Door. Watercolor by Luigi
Vanvitelli and G. P. Panini.

relsome and arrogant Roman nobility, the Church began to supervise the civil administration and government "to help out," as it were and this soon became a permanent arrangement.

The history of the Church as an opponent to state power in Italy and the rest of Europe continues from the High and Late Middle Ages on through the Renaissance until well into modern times. As early as the period of Gregory the Great (590 – 604), the inhabitants of Rome and the surrounding areas (oltre le mura, as it is still called today) considered papal authority to be of a definite civil nature that protected them and afforded some guarantee of security during internal and external conflicts. The sovereignity of the Vatican had in principle been granted according to the Byzantine laws of that time. However, Byzantium was far away, too far for it to wield its power in Rome. The actual exercise of power thus almost inevitably fell to the pontificate in Rome.

Moreover, the Roman bishops had vast landholdings, which were called in the vernacular "the inheritance of St. Peter." The Donation of Constantine made by the Frankish kings in 728 awarded the pontiff the territorial rights and authority of a real head of state. The territory of the Donation had been seized from the Byzantine empire according to the law of might makes right, and as a consequence was endowed with all the attributes of political sovereignity. The area around Sutri, the landholdings already in the hands of the papacy, and further landed properties also taken by force from Byzantium and transferred to the pope together formed an extensive church state. It embraced all of Latium and also the areas called Pentapolis (northeast Italy) and Exarchat (around Ravenna) by the Byzantines – substantial parts of the present-day regions of Umbria, Marches, Romagna and Emilia. The borders of this state more or less marked the civil empire of the pontificate as it remained until the last century or, more accurately, until the foundation of Italy as a nation, which culminated in the occupation of Rome on November 20, 1870. At this time, the pope excommunicated the King of Italy and perceived his own position to be that of an imprisoned victim of violence. Approximately sixty years passed before relations between the Church and state returned to a fair degree of normalcy with the establishment of the present-day state of Vatican City.

V – TOPOGRAPHY OF THE VATICAN TODAY

Pope Boniface VIII (1294–1303) looking down from Loggia della Benedizioni. Codex decorated with miniatures from the Biblioteca Ambrosiana in Milan.

*T*he state of Vatican City is based on the Lateran Treaty signed by the Holy See and the Italian government on February 11, 1929. Recently, some sections in this system of treaties pertaining to economic and civil aspects were revised (i.e., the state is no longer responsible for "adequate" salaries for the pastors, [the congrua], Catholicism is no longer exclusively the "state religion" and religious lessons are now offered only on demand in the schools). A saying that has circulated since then claims "the Tiber has become wider." Editor's note: The Tiber is understood to be a symbolic border between church and state. As is generally known, the treaty of 1929 was made with a fascist political system under the leadership of "cavaliere" Benito Mussolini. The additions and modifications of 1984 were settled with a democratic government, the president of which was — for the first time in postwar Italy — a socialist, Bettino Craxi. Within a very short time, this tiny state has been recognized by almost all governments of the world. (Among the nations who have not recognized the Vatican up to the present are the Soviet Union; in fact, *no* East Bloc country, with the exception of Yugoslavia, has acknowledged the Vatican since the end of World War Two.)

The state of the Vatican covers a total area of 44 hectares (17,8 acres), which is less than one-half square kilometer. This is about the equivalent of a modest country estate. Surrounded on three sides by walls and on the east by Bernini's colonnades, the borders of this state form an irregular pentagon, the longest diagonal of which measures little more than 1,000 meters. The squares and inner courtyards take up about one-third of the ground area and the buildings another third; the rest is covered by gardens. At the most, it takes only two or three minutes to cross the entire state by car. You can cover the length of the borders, which run along Viale Vaticano, in a little more than a half-hour on foot.

The Bronze Door is the most important and also the most impressive entrance to the buildings. Approaching from the Atrium and climbing a slight rise to the Constantine Arch, you come to the Scala Regia and from there proceed to the various salas and the Courtyard of S. Damaso. Official visitors used to be received at this gate, but now they drive past two sentries of the Swiss Guard in parade uniforms and under the bell tower. This entrance is called the Bell Arch (Arco della Campane) because a bell mechanism has been installed in the superstructure above the gate. Its music rings out on church holidays ("awfully early," as many persons affected by it think), and even during the most solemn moments of the liturgy in the basilica or on the piazza. To the left of this entrance and on the left-hand side of the colonnades is the third entrance, "St. Uffizio," so named because it is directly next to the palace which for centuries has been the seat of the oldest and most important congregation of the Catholic church. It became necessary to open an entrance here due to construction of the new audience room commissioned by Paul VI. The building plan for this room was designed by Pier Luigi Nervi, one of the most brilliant of the contemporary engineers to use reinforced concrete. The magnificent sculpture "The Resurrection" created by sculptor Pericle Fazzini adorns the building's interior and is a masterpiece of religious art well worthy of continuing Vatican tradition.

The gate through which the greatest number of visitors enter the Vatican is the gate of St. Anne in Via di Porta Angelica, to the right of the colonnades. Whoever desires to get to know the people who earn their daily bread in the Vatican need only stand at this entrance between 7:30 and 8:30 a.m. This is the "servants' entrance," so to speak, for the blue- and white-collar workers and the government functionaries of this state: the doctors in the health service; the journalists on the Osservatore Romano; the bank clerks at the Istituto per le Opere Religiose (IOR), the "Bank for Religious Works"; and many others who, day after day, go to work within the walls. In keeping with its function, this entrance is only protected by Swiss guards in their plainer, dark blue uniforms without halberds.

Early in the morning is also when all people hoping for a favorable position in the lines in front of the grocery stores appear. Between 8:00 and 11:00 a.m., especially before holidays like Christmas or Easter and the weekends, a huge crowd of people mingles with the heavy traffic of the delivery trucks. Groceries of all sorts are available here; however, the most popular items are the tax-free alcoholic beverages, which really are very cheap (in comparison to the high taxes placed on them by Italy). If liquor sales were expressed in terms of the actual number of Vatican inhabitants, its citizens would be drinking more cognac per day than the average Frenchman per year and more whisky than all the Scots together. The high-proof liquor for sale here is, without exception, of choice quality (which cannot really be said of the wine, which tends to be inferior); this is also true of the beef imported from Holland, or from a socialist country like Hungary which, although it does not recognize the Vatican as a state, certainly appreciates its payments in hard currency.

The pharmacy directly across from the grocery store is open to everybody; identification or special permits are not necessary. Among its steady customers are not only the beneficiaries of the free Vatican health services, but also many people from "outside," since a lot of newly developed medicines become available here before the Italian Ministry of Health gives them its official approval. The Hospitalers, who run the pharmacy, also distill an excellent anise liquor, but advertise it as little as possible. In addition, the monks prepare superb lavender (and other) scents, and are apparently, to this day, the only ones to take back the empty perfume bottles as a deposit on the price of a new bottle. The "homemade" perfumes cost only a fraction of the select French perfumes available in a separate department of the pharmacy.

The St. Anne Gate was named for the small baroque church located to the right of the entrance. This church, under the care of Augustinian monks, is the pope's actual parish church. The pope, as the bishop of Rome and primate of Italy, delegates the bishopric of the city of Rome to a cardinal (the vicar-cardinal) and the state of the Vatican to the vicar-general. The latter is a bishop and sort of archpriest because his parishioners include more cardinals, bishops and prelates than in any other congregation.

The "industrial" and business districts of the state are approached through St. Anne Gate. The barracks of the Swiss Guards and the Gendarmeria and the apartments of the families of several functionaries and employees are located in this intimate little neighborhood where everyone knows and greets everyone else. Sometimes it only takes a single truck loaded with goods for one of the shops at the end of Via del Pellegrino to completely block all traffic. Traffic jams are inevitable (and irritating to the journalists on the Osservatore Romano, who are always in a great rush to get somewhere). Traffic is indeed a big problem here, and despite a speed limit of 30 kilometers per hour, the lowest of any country in the world, no solution is in sight. It is useless to write out tickets and levy fines. Each visitor to this state has some highly-placed protector, who within a few hours, would re-

Baroque ornamentation above the entry to the Lateran Palace, which Pope Sixtus V (1585 – 1590) had built by Domenico Fontana.

quest that the matter be dropped. How could a simple civil servant dare to refuse a cardinal or a prelate such a request? Having friends, or at least one friend, in the Vatican is a maxim of life that is painstakingly observed. Above all, it is important not to incur anyone's displeasure. It is characteristic of this "court" that unpleasant subjects may (and are desired to be) acknowledged only in a tête-à-tête talk. If three or more persons are concerned with the matter, it is better to flatter everybody and put on a show of formal subservience, such behavior, like the jargon of the administration employees, eventually becomes second nature.

The editorial, composing and printing offices of the Osservatore Romano are located at the end of Via del Pellegrinio. The daily newspaper of the Holy See, the Osservatore Romano, is usually designated "semi-official" because it publishes all papal announcements and offical acts of the Curia, as well as current daily events in Rome, Italy and the rest of the world. This daily newspaper, like the state that publishes it, is one of the world's smallest but certainly not one of the least important. It is also one of the oldest in old Europe, founded by a few Catholic laymen in 1861 to help spread the words of the pope. At that time, the crisis in the secular power of the Church was just reaching its climax and the paper was intended to bring the undistorted statements of the pope to the public. The newspaper has no trouble disposing of the rather low circulation: about ten thousand copies, almost all published, are sold to subscribers, not even a thousand copies are sold at newsstands throughout Italy. However, the paper is sold worldwide and is required reading, so to speak, in government offices and consulates. Some copies even reach the Kremlin and the White House.

The number of staff in the editorial department is quite modest: approximately fifteen journalists, almost all of whom come from the laity (as does the head of the editorial staff, who is appointed for an unlimited period). Like everything else in the Vatican, this daily is closely bound to tradition. The paper is produced in crowded, old-fashioned rooms in no way equipped for modern journalism. When John Paul II visited the rooms of the editorial department at the beginning of his pontificate, he was surprised at their miserable state. "You are worse off than the Poles," he reportedly remarked. Although impoverished, the newspaper allows itself a few aristocratic fancies. For example, it is printed on excellent Finnish paper, which is otherwise sold only to Moscow for certain special editions of "Pravda."

Opposite: *The Gate of Death by Giacomo Manzu. Pope John XXIII commissioned the sculptor to build the door, which was dedicated to Don Giuseppe de Luca, a publisher, art critic and librarian who was also a friend of Manzu and John XXIII.*

The statue of the first pope, St. Peter, in the middle aisle in front of the right transept. It probably dates back to the 8th century.

Right: Foreground: *the vault of the Cappella di San Sebastiano adorned with putti.* Background: *a section of the bronze statue of Pope Pius XII (1930-1958), a piece created by Francesco Messina in 1964.*

Far right: *This bronze statue of St. Peter, probably made by Arnolfo da Cambrio, is dressed in papal vestments and a valuable tiara for the Feast of St. Peter and St. Paul on June 29.*

Opposite: *St. Peter's is over 170 meters long and can hold 60,000 people. Owing to the basilica's ingenious construction, the visitor is hardly aware of its overwhelming dimensions.*

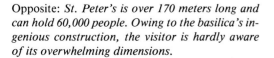

Left: *The dome of the Cappella della Presentazione in the left aisle. The mortal remains of Pope Pius X are in the reliquary under the altar.*

Left center and below: *The gilded coffered dome in the left transept of the Basilica.*
The chapel was completed by Giacomo della Porta during the pontificate of Clement VIII.

Above: *Looking into the dome from the transept. There are sixteen windows in the drum through which sunlight falls.*

Opposite: *Bernini began the bronze canopy in 1624. It was dedicated by Pope Urban VIII on June 28, 1633, on the eve of the Feast of St. Peter and St. Paul. The bronze melted for the canopy came from the entrance hall of the Pantheon. Michelangelo's dome consists of four magnificent vaults resting on four huge pentagonal piers that measure 71 meters around.*

Overleaf: *The left transept and Bernini's canopy over the high altar, as seen from the drum of Michelangelo's dome.*

Above: *Pope John Paul II during Mass at the papal altar (called Altare della Confessione) made by Maderno.*

Opposite: *Looking into Michelangelo's dome with the apse. In the background, the scene around St. Peter's throne. Above it, the gilded rays of the stucco halo, framed by putti and angels amidst the clouds. They surround the symbol of the Holy Ghost portrayed in the window. This splendid work of Baroque art was created by Gian Lorenzo Bernini between 1656 and 1665.*

Above left: *Priests during a celebration of the Mass with the pope. They are standing in front of a statue of the canonized Empress Helena, the mother of Emperor Constantine. The five-meter-tall statue is the work of Andrea Bolgi (1630-1639). It stands in one of the niches created by Bernini at the foot of the piers in Michelangelo's dome.*

Above: *Bernini's impressive bronze canopy is 25 meters high. It rises above the gilded bronze cathedra of St. Peter which was also executed by Bernini. The spiral columns are reminiscent of the columns that separated the sacral area of the medieval basilica for over a thousand years.*

Overleaf: *A Mass under the bronze canopy. The light streaming in from the dome and the spotlights present the resplendent architecture in its full beauty.*

Right: *Stucco ceiling by Martino Ferrabosco in Maderno's entrance hall. It contains Pope Paul V's coat of arms from the fifteenth year of his pontificate.*

Below: *One of the sixteen panels of the Holy Door, portraying the Crucifixion. It was made by Vico Consorti from Sienna for the 1950 holy year under Pope Pius XII.*

Below right: *The equestrian statue of Emperor Constantine, made by Bernini in 1670. It stands in front of a stucco curtain that evokes the impression of damask interwoven with gold.*

Above far right: *One of the Baroque angels on Bernini's canopy above the high altar.*

Right: *A section of Maderno's entrance hall with a statue of Caritas and stucco work by Ambrogio Bonvicino.*

Opposite: *The famous Pietà in the Cappella della Pietà, one of Michelangelo's early works carved from 1499 to 1500. Jean de Bilberes, a French cardinal and a legate of Charles VIII at the court of Pope Alexander VI, commissioned Michelangelo to carve this piece.*

*The crucifixion of St. Peter, one of four Roma-
nesque marble reliefs decorating the ciborium
Pope Stixtus IV had built above the altar of the
old Constantinian Basilica in 1479. It was later
stored in the Grotte Vaticane, but will supposedly
be re-installed.*

Right: *Sarcophagus of Pope Bonifacius VIII, the
successor of Pope Coelestine V, in the Grotte
Vaticane. This great pope celebrated the first holy
year in 1300. He founded the Università della Sa-
pienza in Rome and was a patron of Giotto.*

Opposite: *A part of the mausoleum of the Cat-
enians in the Roman necropolis, discovered during excavations under the Constantinian Basilica
between 1939 and 1949. It is not far from the
grave of St. Peter behind the mysterious G Wall (a
hiding place where the mortal remains of a person
now held to be St. Peter were interred in the wall
in 315).*

The paper appears in the afternoon — usually a bit late, because the Secretariat of State takes its time with the "official" notices. Until recently, the paper was considered to be a prime example of journalistic composure, above the usual lust for a headline or a scoop, even if it concerned the Curia. This composure has sometimes led to paradoxical results. For example, the Osservatore mentioned the official ratification of the Lateran Treaty in an unimposing notification consisting of only five lines of print: "This afternoon, a treaty between the Holy See and Italy was signed in the Papal Hall of the Apostolic Palace. A financial agreement is included in the terms of the Treaty." That was all that was written about this historical moment! When Rome was placed under the supreme command of German Nazis during World War II, the military command posted two SS men on Piazza S. Pietro. They were intended as a warning to the Vatican not to shelter any wanted persons, Allied soldiers who had fled imprisonment or fighters in the Resistance. The newspaper could not ignore this, but also did not wish to overemphasize it, so it simply wrote: "As indicated by some Roman newspapers, the German Kommandant has placed patrols on the border between the state of Vatican City and Italy."

It is said that the Osservatore is the world's least often read and most often quoted newspaper, which could well be true. An observation by a Vatican undersecretary of state, Monsignore Tardini, sums up the paper's reputation. Pitying a nuncio in some isolated,uneventful country or other, he observed, "Just imagine how bored the poor man must be — he reads the Osservatore from front to back!"

For quite a long time, several small-format weeklies have also been published in various languages: French, English, Spanish, German, Portuguese and others. Since the election of John Paul II there has even been a monthly magazine written in Polish with a circulation of over 100,000. (The copies are sent immediately to the Polish episcopate, but not without first passing through the hands of the Polish censors.) Furthermore, there is an Italian-language weekly paper, called "dei parroci" (meaning approximately "the latest from the parish") by the editors, and a weekly paper, "L'Osservatore della Domenica," reserved exclusively for news which would appear under the heading of "miscellaneous" in other papers.

Opposite: *A panel from the magnificent Gate of Death by the sculptor Giacomo Manzu. Pope John XXIII, who died in 1963, is portrayed here kneeling in prayer for his famous encyclica on peace, "pacem in terris." He wrote it at the beginning of his pontificate.*

Guglielmo Marconi, the inventor of the radio, installed Radio Vatican in person. The original technical installations were located in a restored medieval tower in the Vatican, but today, only the management is housed there. The technical equipment and the production staff have been moved; the technical installations are now at Santa Maria della Galeria, about twenty ilometers outside the city boundaries of Rome, and the production department is located at the end of Via della Conciliazione near Castel S. Angelo. The broadcasting is directed by the Society of Jesus (the Jesuits) who indisputably possess a talent for organization and professional know-how in this area. The station broadcasts news throughout the world, even to regions where hardly anything is known about Catholicism and the pope, or where the broadcasts can only be listened to secretly. In addition to the task of publicizing the pope's pronouncements worldwide, Radio Vatican endeavors to record all papal speeches completely and exactly, during trips as well as during pastoral visits and at audiences.

The Holy See also controls a press and information office. It is situated directly on the Vatican border at the intersection of Via della Conciliazione with the edge of the square named for Pius XII. The waiting room (still in the hands of the Italians) faces St. Peter's Square. The press office serves accredited journalists who, with infallible regularity, complain about the information provided. Although probably no other institution is more reserved than the Holy See, journalists often feel its discretion is a camouflage tactic to be penetrated either intuitively or according to their ideological viewpoints. Nevertheless, texts of papal speeches are distributed here as communiqués and, in rare cases – for example during synods or on the occasion of a new encyclical – events and important documents are interpreted. The recently appointed director of the press and information office, Dr. Joaquin Navarro-Vals of Spain, is a Catholic layman.

A little over a year ago, a fourth communications medium was established in the Vatican, namely a television studio. For the time being, the studio is content to film the pope's trips and make video cassettes that are competently narrated in many languages and sold throughout the world. The subject of the first cassette was John Paul II's pilgrimage to Lourdes in mid-1983. The absolute best-seller has proven to be the cassette of his trip to Canada.

The Vatican Fire Department's coat of arms.

A notable number of publications are produced directly by the Vatican's polylingual printing office ("la Polyglotta"). A cultural institution with a long tradition, it uses various typefaces in the Greek, Hebraic, Arabic, Assyrian, Cyrillic, Coptic, Armenian, Etruscan and Georgian alphabets, mainly for the small liturgical pamphlets and libretti distributed in St. Peter's before each celebration of the Mass. "La segreta," the office's secret chamber, is located in a small room at the printer's office and is open only to those who swear to absolute secrecy about the work they do there. The galley proofs of the encyclicas, pastorals and other announcements, the contents of which may only be made public on special orders, are typeset here. Although a lot of rumors can be cooked up in the Vatican as a consequence of so much secrecy (a problem characteristic of all religious communities) the aura of confidentiality is respected, not only with regard to the foreign language printer's office, but in the case of other state secrets, too, such as appointments or transfers; that is, for proceedings in which all participants depend on the utmost discretion — for those who announce appointments, so that they will not be the object of constant, irritating observation and for those who may possibly be appointed, so that their appointment will not be cancelled at the last minute, as has sometimes occurred when a planned appointment became known too early.

Another medium of communication is Libreria Editrice Vaticana, the state-owned book publisher. Its offices are located in the Polyglotta building with the editorial departments of the Vatican newspapers and other publications. Just as Radio Vatican is controlled by the Jesuits, so is the Osservatore and foreign language printer's offices and their managements in the hands of the Salesians. Indeed, at the Vatican functions and services in the civil administrations and the Secretariat of State are unmistakably distributed, even though these assignments have never been explicitly defined. The telephone system is the domain of the Sisters of St. Paul. Thus, whoever wishes to be connected to an inside line in the Vatican by one of the friendly female voices at the switchboard is well-advised to address the operators as "Sister," and not as "Miss." The Society of St. Paul the Apostle was originally entrusted with the television station, but at a decisive moment young lay people from the association "Comunione e Liberazione" were able to gain control of this responsibility.

Pope Pius VII giving the benediction to the crowd on Easter Sunday, April 8, 1919. Especially interesting are the "flabella" (fans of white feathers) containing the papal coat of arms and the clergyman throwing two tickets of indulgence, the absolution of penance for sins granted by the Church, to the crowd. English lithograph by Bridgens from 1820.

Of late, a certain pluralism has even been observed in the appointment of the editor-in-chief at the Osservatore. A prelate who suggested several persons for the job was supposedly given to understand that he could not nominate certain journalists because they belonged to Comunione e Liberazione and that, to prevent being accused of favoritism, it would be advisable for him to suggest someone from Catholic Action ("Azione Cattolica"). It is thus to be suspected that, irrespective of the undisputed professional capabilities of the young Spanish journalist eventually chosen, membership in Opus Dei was not the least factor that influenced his appointment to the management of the press office.

The national origins of the prelates are being considered to an increasing extent in appointments to the Curia. Since the Second Vatican Council, the internationalization of the Curia has proceeded steadily, it being only natural that more and more people familiar with the problems and specific situations of the various linguistic regions would be required. Perhaps the climax of this development was the election of John Paul II, a Polish prelate, which led to the usual malcontent criticism, but also the defense that the capability to fulfill a certain task and not nationality is the most important qualification. The Curia has always thought more in terms of universality than of nationality. Be that as it may, the importance of the national origins of single dignitaries in the upper levels of the Curia is constantly becoming clearer: if the Secretary of State had not been Italian, then a Spaniard could not have been appointed as his deputy. The number of prelates from North and South America and Africa is steadily growing.

It is impossible to know the Vatican — not to mention to establish relations with the Vatican — without possessing the "Annuario Pontifico" (the "Papal Yearbook" of the hierarchy in the Catholic Church). For dealings with the Vatican, it is as essential as using a good dictionary when speaking a foreign language whose vocabulary one has not completely mastered. Published regularly at the beginning of the year, the Annuario is an elegant folio of more than two thousand closely spaced pages, bound in cardinal red cloth, in an edition of twenty-five thousand copies. To those who know how to read it properly, it contains scores of names of people and places, and reveals the organization and structure of the Church institution, and thus all of its varied historical, apostolic, social, cultural, technical and missionary elements.

VI – ADMINISTRATION AT THE VATICAN

The Gallery of Maps in the Vatican palaces.

*T*he State of Vatican City levies no taxes. Looked at from this perspective, it could be mistaken for the most socialist (if not the most communist) country in the world. Surplus value has not only been eliminated, it cannot possibly arise, because the State produces no consumer goods. Certain other small nations have at least some sort of economy, but not the Vatican. The major income it receives is comprised of the rents from apartments throughout Rome, above all near the Vatican; these rents are determined according to the Italian law for protection of tenants. Most of the apartments have been let to employees of the Vatican belonging both to the clergy and laity. Other sources of revenue are the portfolio of stocks (consisting mainly of shares in non-Italian companies) and the sales of stamps and products from the Vatican coin and medallion mint. According to an agreement with the Italian government, the Vatican is entitled to mint several million coins in Italian currency privately, provided the coins correspond exactly to real Italian specie in alloying, dimensions and weight. Vatican coins, as opposed to Italian coins, disappear into coin collections and as souvenirs for tourists within a few months of issue. Yet another source of income is generated by the entrance fees to the Vatican Museums which, despite the sky-high upkeep expenditure show a positive balance (in contrast to the very expensive subsidies necessary for the maintenance of the Vatican Library and the Archives, which are devoted above all to restoring the precious books and documents stored there. From the beginning, the Church has valued the cultural importance of these institutions so highly that it has always conferred the rank of cardinal on the prefect of the Library of the Holy Church of Rome.)

The authorities at the Vatican have to think up a good many ways to raise the funds necessary for maintenance, restoration, expansion and improvements, as overhead costs are already so high there is no money left for extrabudgetary expenditures. To give a current example: the present librarian, Cardinal Stickler, decided to initiate a great publishing venture of high cultural value. Together with other editors, and supported by sponsors, especially from Germany, Japan and the United States, he is publishing a series of facsimiles of the codices intended to comprise one hundred volumes. (Some, such as the codex of Ptolemy, have already appeared in a perfectly reproduced limited edition.) Substantial amounts of capital were invested initially, yet the editors and sponsors have delivered such convincing results that a large number of the volumes have already been sold on a subscription basis.

The Library's net profits must be considerable, as the enlargements to the building, including the necessary and ingenious air conditioning and ventilation systems, are now being built. The authorities at the Vatican Museums have had a similar success with the renovation of the Sistine Chapel: the restoration of Michelangelo's frescos is being financed by a Japanese company based in Rome. In return, they have been granted the exclusive film and photograph rights for a whole decade. Whoever views the chapel after completion of the general overhaul in a few years will face an entirely "new" Michelangelo, not the master of dramatic gestures in colors turned brownish from dampness and dust whom most of us know today. Even today it is spoken of as the restoration of the century, and art critics will have to review the results just now starting to appear.

Another source of revenue comes from the sale of Vatican stamps. Hardly a pilgrim misses the chance to mail a few postcards with the stamp of Poste Vaticane on St. Peter's Square. These stamps, like Vatican-minted coins, are subject to the condition that their value correspond to that of Italian postage. The majority of these stamps also disappear in stamp collectors' albums, and the long lines of professional dealers who gather at the issuing counters to buy whole sheets of them and first day postmarks have been a familiar picture up to the present. At times polemic accusations by philatelists that the Vatican was issuing too many stamps and thus curbing the increase in their value could be heard.

The Vatican Museums are an important part of the "sacri palazzi." As mentioned above, their nucleus is comprised of the interior decorations commissioned by the popes of the Renaissance period as well as the works of art in the rooms, corridors and gardens collected to complete the interior and exterior. In the course of the eighteenth century, the systematic classification of the antiques of Roman origin was begun and special rooms were created for them. This proceeding is being repeated for the remaining works of art in this century. No other institution in the world can compare to the Vatican Museums with regard to the variety of exhibits from all epochs and cultures.

Opposite: *Street to the north of the Sistine Chapel. It leads from Cortile della Sentinella to Piazza del Forno, and continues under the name of Via della Fondamenta along the right-hand side of the Basilica.*

The north side of the Sistine Chapel. The gable used to serve defence purposes. The supporting piers were added by Pirro Ligorio in the 16th century.

Left: General view of the papal palaces around the Courtyard of the Belvedere. In the foreground is the Sistine Chapel. Grouped in a horseshoe shape in the middle is the long Gallery of Maps, along which Stradone dei Giardini runs to the left. In the background are the Library and the Pio-Clementine Museum; to the right and opposite the other gallery is the long corridor called Lapidaria Gallery.

The view from the terrace of the Basilica looking toward the Palazzo del Santo Uffizio; in the foreground, the dome of the Sacristy. The palace, which dates from the time of Pope Pius V (1566-1572), has a large inner courtyard, an entrance hall and a loggia.

Right: The three rows of loggias that rise above the Courtyard of San Damaso are the ingenious work of Bramante and Raphael. In the background are the left Bernini colonnade and the slope of Gianicolo Hill.

Behind the Cortile della Sentinella (the Courtyard of the Guard) lies Piazza della Zecca. The small gate opens onto Via delle Fondamenta and Via del Governatorato and leads to the Vatican Gardens.

Left: *View of the large and small domes of the chapels.*

Overleaf: *The start of a new day. It will not be long until the Vatican squares and corners pulse with life.*

The Cortile del Belvedere, designed by Bramante, is the Vatican's largest inner courtyard. Its sides are formed by buildings built during Pope Pius IV's pontificate in the 15th century. A large, bowl-shaped fountain stands in the middle.

Left: *The Gate of Pope Paul V leads into the Courtyard of the Belvedere; from here the road leads to the Door of St. Anne and the Via del Pellegrino.*

Above right: *Partial view of the Palazzo della Cancelleria. After 1521, the Cancelleria Apostolica, the papal chancellory, was located here. Its tasks are now carried out by the Secretariat of State.*

Right: *Cardinal Raffaele Riaro had the Palazzo della Cancelleria built not far from Piazza Navona, under the guidance of Bramante, from 1485 to 1520.*

The Swiss Guard is on duty at the Bronze Door.
This entrance to the Apostolic Palace was created
by Marino Ferrabosco and Giovanni Basanzio in
1619. The bronze door leaves were added by Bernini in 1667.

Right: The bathroom of Cardinal Bibbiena in the
Segretaria di Stato (the Secretariat of State) is not
open to the public. Bibbiena was born in 1470 and
died in 1520 in Rome; he was a plenipotentiary,
papal legate and diplomat.

The Belvedere of Pope Innocent VIII, built by Jacopo da Pietrasanta according to a design by Antonio Pollajolo between 1484 and 1487.

Left: *View of the Vatican Gardens from Stradone de Giardini, a path which starts at the Cortile della Corazze. The statue in the foreground is a modern work of art.*

The new audience hall designed by the architect
Pier Luigi Nervi and built from 1964 to 1971. A
part of the large room for the faithful lies below
ground level so that the hall does not impair the
view of the adjoining buildings.

Opposite: *The audience hall can hold up to 12,000
people. Nervi's building is very bold. Behind the
papal throne stands a huge statue of Christ resur-
rected by Pericle Fazzini, a sculptor born in Grot-
tamare (also the birthplace of the great Pope Sixtus V).*

The view from Ponto di Castel Sant'Angelo to the dome of St. Peter's. In the foreground, the church of Santo Spirito in Sasso, built for Saxon pilgrims.

Right: *Partial view of the Vatican walls at the entrance to the Museums in spring.*

Fortifications of Pope Paul III and Pope Urban VIII along the Vatican walls. One of the two corner towers belonging to the former surrounding walls of Pope Nicholaux V can be seen. It was restored by Pope John XXIII.

Left: *The borders of the Vatican state correspond largely with the walls Pope Leo IV had built in the 9th century to defend the Vatican from the Saracens. The walls were enlarged and fortified under Popes Paul III and Urban VIII during the Renaissance and the Baroque era.*

These exhibits are displayed in an area of approximately 30,000 square meters, which does not even include the space in the small gardens and inner courtyards. During the eighteenth century every pope attended to the museums, and this dedication bore fruit — an unusual plant, still growing even now. This is also true of the popes in the latter half of the twentieth century. Paul VI, for example, an extraordinarily well-educated man with an excellent knowledge of art, added to the collection about seven hundred works of modern religious art donated by about two hundred artists throughout the world. It is especially significant that these works were donated; for centuries the Church has boasted of its patronage of the arts and now, suddenly, it finds itself dependent on patrons, as the purchase of works of art requires an enormous amount of liquid assets no longer available in practice today. However, the spirit of tradition has been well preserved in this area, and it is considered a great honor for any artist to have his work represented in these museums. It is not easy to be accepted here. Of course, widely recognized artists have fewer problems, but it is more difficult for artists who do not yet have an international reputation. Many, particularly hobby artists, give the pope their works during audiences or stops on his journeys. Maybe they hope that the products of their art and crafts will end up in the museums, but this is not the case. At best, they land in the "Floreria," a sort of "funny flower collection" where even furniture from the Vatican-owned apartments is stored.

There are exceptions extremely rare, but most members of the Curia admit they "don't have time" for relevant reading or to attend cultural events. At the most, they go to a concert now and again, but otherwise are too preoccupied for "overwork."

Nevertheless, even if it cannot be said that Vatican prelates have the requisite "highbrow" education, the Vatican promotes a "cultural policy."

A short while ago the pope created a commission for cultural affairs. He had already entrusted a bishop from the vicariate of Rome with this pastoral job, but the Curia feels a certain mistrust of persons engaged in the cultural sector that can hardly be put into words. They are used to a strict hierarchy of offices, and a real intellectual could never be fully integrated into such a system, even if he desired to adapt himself to it. For example, Charles Moeller, a literary critic known throughout

Opposite: *View from a walkway leading to the Sistine Chapel, the inner courtyard and the Borgia Palace.*

Europe who concentrated on the relation between literature and faith, lived for years in the Vatican and wrote works of fundamental importance for the Church. Regardless of his significance, hardly anybody at the Vatican knew him in that context. He was just Monsignore Moeller to them. It was the same with Marshall McLuhan, who was a member of the "Commissione per le Communicazione sociale" for many years but who could never attend its meetings because the trip from his native Canada to Rome was supposedly too expensive to subsidize.

Cultural activities here are always bound to the initiative and assertiveness of individual persons; they can occur only if someone in an important position of responsibility is convinced of their worth. The exhibitions organized by the managements of the library and the museums are thus important and also of an unusually high standard. It is also notable, in this respect, that the Vatican has loaned extremely valuable objects of art (for example, the Apollo Belvedere) for exhibitions in various cities in the United States.

For about the last 10 to 12 years, the Vatican's economic problems have appeared in the headlines of newspapers around the world, owing largely to some unfortunate affairs. John Paul II has commissioned a board of fourteen cardinals to analyse the financial problems of the Holy See as its balances have been going deeper into the red ("a constantly increasing unfavorable balance," as bankers would say) ever since the pontificate of Paul VI. Ironically, it was Paul VI who gave instructions to dispose of numerous portfolios of stocks from companies that had policies irreconcilable with the social principles of the Church.

The financial status of the Vatican is a complicated affair, one not easily comprehended and increasingly the target of public controversy. Yet, the Vatican and its institutions, even the Holy See, can no longer ignore the necessity of dealing with financial matters. If one considers the hundreds of congregations to which about eight thousand missionaries (monks as well as lay persons) throughout the world belong and who have to be supported suitably, it automatically becomes clear that there is no way around financial dealings of all sorts.

With the confirmation of the Lateran Treaty of 1929 between the Vatican and Italy, the Holy See was rewarded about one billion lire in reparation for the vast wealth of the Church confiscated by the Italian government around 1870. Three quarters of this amount was paid in cash and the rest in securities at five percent interest. Pius XI created a special office consisting exclusively of lay persons to administer this fortune, and they have apparently re-invested the existing capital to increase yields. Furthermore, the Holy See can count on the contributions of Catholics worldwide given under the motto of "a penny for St. Peter" ("Obolo di San Pietro"). The pope also receives single gifts of money and legacies.

The Vatican administration is a matter in itself. It is remarkably awkward, although it is not really clear what prevents it from functioning more flexibly and simply. First, there is the "Prefettura degli Affari Economici della Santa Sede" (Ecnomic Department of the Holy See); then the "Administrazione del Patrimonio della Sede Apostolica" (Administration of the Property of the Apostolic See), both of which were founded by Paul VI; and finally the "Istituto per le Opere de Religione" (IOR, the Institute for Religious Works). The prefecture could be characterized as a sort of audit office, so far as it is permissible to use a definition pertaining to a normal government for an institution in the Vatican. The "Prefettura" controls the fiscal policies of the various departments of government and the congregations, informs the pope about their financial status and reports on the financial situation of the Holy See. The Administration of Property (APSA) is responsible for managing all possessions of the Holy See as well as for the support of the Vatican employees; in other words, the members of the Curia and of the various congregations. However, it is not to be equated directly with the corresponding bodies in secular governments. The IOR, founded by Leo XIII in 1887 to administer religious works (i.e. endowments and donations) and changed to a corporate body according to law by Pius XII in 1942, protects and administers all revenues appropriated for use in religious works, which are for the most part contributed by congregations and religious orders. The seat of the IOR is located in the fortified bastion of Nicholas V. Except for the top management, the personnel are all lay persons. All deposits are administered on a trust basis because this institution issues neither statements of account nor savings account books, only a numbered index sheet that reveals the persons having signatory power and the species of foreign currency paid in. The logical conclusion can be drawn that the Istituto per le Opere di Religione is a type of national bank comparable to those of France, the United States, Italy and Great Britain, even though it is not designated as such and also does not carry out the usual functions of a bank (i.e., buying and selling money).

Nevertheless, the cardinal-prefect for economic affairs recently reconfirmed the complete independence of the IOR from the Holy See at a meeting of the fourteen cardinals — a statement that is difficult to understand in light of the Institute's involvement with the bankruptcy of Roberto Calvi's Banco Ambrosiano private bank in Milan. (Calvi was later found hanged under a bridge over the Thames.) The IOR held such a large number of shares that it supposedly incurred losses of 500 billion lire (which is equal to the value of its portfolio of stocks) when the Banco Ambrosiano failed. The trial led to much criticism of the Holy See regardless of the emphatic assurance that the Institute was independent. An agreement was eventually reached to relieve the stockholders' financial losses as far as possible, yet at the same time any and all responsibility for the financial drama was specifically denied.

Two opposing opinions have developed in the Vatican since this affair: one is against any type of compensation payments on principle and the other is prepared to make certain concessions with regard to payment of damages, although its members also vehemently deny any moral or legal guilt. At the time, the cardinal secretary of state and even the pontiff himself inclined to the latter opinion, and it was said that the pontiff, who had little knowledge of financial matters and was not well acquainted with the situation at the Institute, aimed at a composition, even if this step were to mean having to sell some property. A committee of six persons, inlcuding three representatives from the IOR and three from the Italian national bank, finally investigated the situation. This led in the end to the IOR releasing 433 billion lire from its own reserves as compensation.

The economic board of fourteen cardinals published a carefully researched final report after their last study that contains extremely alarming figures about the Vatican state's financial situation. In 1984 the deficit already amounted to over 58 billion lire and the commission predicted a 63 billion lire deficit for 1985. Only the government building had a credit balance of about half a billion lire. The deficit has to be added to the current costs for the Curia and the nunciatures, that is, for the maintenance of 1,817 people presently working at the Vatican as well as 911 retired employees. The cardinal-prefect also disclosed a larger number of statistics in his public communiqué than has ever before been made known. For example, he mentioned that Radio Vatican has a deficit of almost fifteen billion lire.

To absorb at least some of the losses, the revenues from "pennis for St. Peter" have already been taken into account. They amounted to about 55 billion lire in 1984. Most of the deficit was made good by "time reserve assets." Due to the fiscal difficulties, efforts have been made to introduce a systematic austerity program with "controlled poverty" ("povertà controllata"), but there is a bottom limit to financial needs that cannot be lowered further, and it is certainly out of the question to restrict the apostolic mission of the pope for such profane reasons. Even so, John Paul II's great activism has brought forth an unusually complicated machinery of organization that has naturally resulted in higher costs. Since he has taken office, there has been more work, and more work has its price. An attempt was made to avoid increasing the number of employees to do this work, but that proved to be infeasible: overtime was more expensive than hiring new personnel. Out of fear of additional costs, no one has yet confronted the unavoidable changes and renewals necessary in the bureaucratic and technical hierarchies, even though everybody knows that the cost of maintaining an inefficient organization is much higher than it is for an appropriate system.

The State of Vatican City is a sovereign corporate body according to international law. The head of state is the pope and all powers – legislative, jurisdictional and executive – are invested in his person. Legislation is incumbent upon the pope or is delegated by him to the Papal Committee of State ("Pontificia Commissione per lo Stato"). The government is in charge of the regulations for implementation. Executive power has been transferred to a "delgato speciale" assisted by an advisory council ("consulta"), which consists of twenty-four lay members and is chaired by a "delegato speciale" (that is, a special representative).

The scope of the Secretariat's duties within the government includes affairs of general importance, labor and civil law problems of the Vatican "citizens," merchandise traffic, the mail and telegraph services, the security and information services, the issuing of stamps, coins and medallions

Key for the statue of St. Peter (1575). In the "Museo del tesoro di San Pietro" (Treasury of St. Peter).

and the General Accounting Office. Several specialized subdivisions of the Secretariat supervise the monuments, museums and galeries, technical services such as Radio Vatican, and the health service for employees. At the top of the jurisdictional branch of government stand a single judge, a court of first instance, a court of appeals ("Corte di Appello") and a court of cassation ("Corte di Cassazione"), analogous to the structure of the Italian judicial system. All instances administer justice in the name of the pontiff.

As in all other communities of the world, not a single citizen in the Vatican is not in some way personally concerned with the administrative machinery: the renewal of a passport or shopping permit, gasoline vouchers, the purchase of a car, the confirmation of residence or the contract for the worker who is supposed to repair the water heater in the bathroom — no matter what you want you have to petition for it in person at Government Palace. On the other hand, bureaucratic red tape is kept to a minimum in many areas, if only because everybody has a personal, direct contact to somebody in the administration who will help speed up the bureaucratic process considerably. But let no one think that this condition is entirely idyllic. It is, for example, incomprehensible why some of the services in the Vatican are so cheap or even free of charge, whereas others are much more expensive than in the Italian government despite all its taxes and rates. The carwash at the parking lot costs twice as much at the Vatican as in other parts of Italy, and having a light bulb changed or minor repairs made are even more expensive. You are forced to adapt to this somehow: for example, if the plumber repairs your water heater after work illicitly, in return you do him a personal favor at another time (somewhat reminiscent of economic life in socialist countries).

A specialized dealer for clothing and textiles (and for some other articles of daily use, such as clocks, lighters and transistor radios) is located in the basement of Government Palace. All the goods are of choice quality. People familiar with Rome and looking for certain articles — for example an English trench coat, Austrian loden, Scottish kilts or sweaters and scarves of pure cashmere — shop here. On the average, prices are about thirty percent lower than those in the boutiques on Via Condotti. The place is frequented by the Vatican proletariat, so to speak, whereas the bourgeois and aristocracy shop in the stores around Government Palace.

The Vatican has an exemplary health service for its citizens and employees, especially in comparison to the Italian system, which is in a sad state. The Medical Service ("Fondo Assistenza Sanitaria," FAS) is equipped with its own outpatient clinics in the Vatican and has made agreements with many specialists and good hospitals for inpatient treatment. Neither first aid stations nor hospitals are located in the Vatican itself, only a physician on emergency duty who is however on twenty-four hour call and can arrive within two or three minutes, owing to the short distances in this state. The excellently organized emergency service run by the Order of the Knights of Malta helps out at public audiences and other appearances of the pope that attract large crowds of people. Their ambulances have been equipped with the latest equipment, and their personnel are also first class.

The Vatican train station is probably the ugliest and saddest-looking building in the State. It can only be hoped that this building will soon be torn down (along with the graceless Government Palace) to make more space and complement the Vatican's artistic heritage. There is hardly any railway traffic to speak of, as the train station and its direct connection to Trastevere station in Rome were, when built, really no more than a political declaration of intention: a confirmation that the state, founded in 1929, had its own rail connection. Heavy goods, such as paper rollers for the Osservatore Romano or marble slabs for repairs in the basilica, are still delivered to the station, but the only product ever shipped from the station according to my knowledge, is a statue of John Paul II created by the sculptor Minguzzi for Cracow, it stood out in the open for weeks before being sent off. Within recent memory, only two passenger trains have arrived here: the first, when John XXIII set off on a pilgrimage to Loreto and Assisi shortly before the Second Council was convened (thus, starting the era of papal journeys which Paul VI continued and which John Paul II has made into the most notable characteristic of his pontificate); and the second, when two cars from the special train "Settobello" carried John Paul II, his entourage and journalists to the "Stazione Termini" train station in Rome, a "journey" of fifteen kilometers at the most. Since 1976, a helicopter landing field has been in operation in the inner courtyard of one of the bastions located near the tower named for John XXIII. The pope uses an Italian air force helicopter to embark on his journeys throughout the world from Fiumicino airport and for trips in Italy, as well as for commuting back and forth from Castel Gandolfo to St. Peter's Square in the summer. A very carefully worded agreement regulating the use of the helicopter guarantees that the contracting partner Italy incurs no additional costs by providing this service.

The different centuries and cultures are constantly colliding in this small state. For example, the helicopter landing field, which is made of reinforced concrete, was built in the heart of medieval fortifications. Pius IV's small residence is a jewel of the Renaissance situated next to extremely modern buildings, whereas the train station is half "Egyptian" and half Art Nouveau. This variety, and the range of the different epochs, are especially obvious when you take a walk through the gardens (which incidentally appear much larger than they actually are because they are crisscrossed by a confusing network of paths and include the hilly part of the Vatican). Many a prelate who cannot afford a summer vacation and many Monsignori kept here by business seek rest and relaxation in these gardens during the summer months. During the hot time of year they are the only place where you can catch a bit of air. While the old oaks, a few large parasol pines, the chestnut oaks and the bushes cannot give relief from the heat, they do at least provide shade and, in the evening hours, a whisper of wind.

The great history and the minor stories of the Vatican are reflected in the place names. In addition to the names of popes and names tending to denote function (for example, "Cortile della Sentinella" or "dei Pappagalli"), "arcadian" names predominate, such as "Viale del bosco" (Forest Street), "Viale degli ulivi" (Olive Tree Street), "Largo della capanna Cinese" (Pagoda Square) and "Piazza del forno" (Baking Oven Square). There is even a "Viale dello Sport" – not because sports are valued particularly highly here, but rather because some tennis courts and a boccia lane are located on the adjoining field. The boccia lane has been closed down, however, since the elder generation of monsignori no longer cavorts here. There are even a basketball court and a badminton court here (although I cannot remember ever having seen anyone play there).

VII – MODERN TOPOGRAPHY

St. Peter's Square as depicted in a fresco by Paris Nogari (1589 – 1590) in the Istituto Massimo, Rome.

As you are constantly aware of the huge dome, so are you aware of the powerful rushing or quiet trickling of the fountains when you walk around the grounds. Supposedly several hundred fountains of all imaginable sizes and shapes are to be found here. Some have potable water and some, it is said, provide curative waters. As proof of this, the visitor is referred to the inscriptions on memorial stones such as those found on the fountain at the beginning of Via del Pellegrino or the one on Via delle Fondamenta. People filling containers and bottles here to replenish their supply of water are a common sight and during the summer months it is only natural to refresh yourself with a sip of fountain water — even the Monsignore strolling solemnly along and the handicapped retired man do so.

The garden landscaping is an excellent indicator of how contemporary taste, which always conflicts with the dominant style, slowly changes with time. An unrestrained will to create given free rein is evident in the construction of both the small and large fountains here that keep the gardeners very busy. The Baroque and Classic styles prevail in the designs of the fountains. A Monisgnore well-known for his biblical research, and famed for his quick-wittedness, is supposed to have said once in reference to the numerous fountains and the meager Vatican salaries, "You can easily starve to death in the Vatican, but you will never ever die of thirst."

Fontana della galeria has attained a certain degree of fame among the countless fountains as a small masterpiece of the Baroque's wealth of ideas. In the middle of a basin in which papyrus flourishes, a lead model of a man-of-war has been set up. Numerous jets of water spout from the cannon embrasures. Its Latin inscription translates as, "The pope's machines of war do not spit fire, but rather water, in order to extinguish the flames of war." Only a few visitors discover this fountain because it is hidden in an out-of-the-way corner.

Spring almost always comes early to Rome, usually a bit ahead of the calendar. Moreover, the Vatican Hill area lies on the leeward side of the wind, protected from the cold blasts that blow down from the snow-covered heights, so most of the plants bud as early as February and are in full bloom before the meadows turn into seas of flowers. During past decades the gardens were meticulously kept and the gravel paths always neat; blowing leaves or grass cuttings were never to be seen. This has since changed. Recently, in addition to the tidy flower beds, there have been a lot of wild plants, much to the joy of the Sisters of St. Martha, who pick the wildflowers for their chapel and for table decorations for the monsignori. A certain Brother Pharmacist is even happier and collects herbs in such intensely concentrated attention that any stroller who sees him from afar gladly gives him a wide berth, so as not to disturb him.

It is usually quiet in the gardens, except during Holy Week, when young people from different Catholic groups come down the way of the Cross and wait to pray with the pope in front of the Grotta di Lourdes. This grotto is an exact small-scale reproduction and John Paul II celebrates Mass here for pilgrims and his "fellow citizens" of the Vatican during the nice time of the year.

There is neither a cafe, nor a bar, nor even a restaurant in Vatican City where people can meet informally. Visitors must content themselves with a few coin-operated automatic coffee machines. A sort of canteen serves lunch to those employed directly in the Vatican, and there is also one for the police. In addition there is a food service and a regular bar for the members of the Swiss Guard. The Hospice of St. Maria, or, more accurately, the papal "Ospizio Santa Maria" is looked upon as the "Vatican Hilton" and affords rooms for the monsignori of the Curia who do not have their own apartments. It is run by "suore vicenziane," who provide miracles of hospitality at (subsidized) prices that are cheap even for members of the religious orders with their small incomes. Until recently, a complete meal including table wine and coffe cost only three dollars.

The Vatican has approximately 650 "true" inhabitants, including officially registered inhabitants who live outside the walls. Exact figures are not available because the number of "functionaries" fluctuates constantly with the changing positions. Somewhat more than half, or about 350 Vatican citizens, carry a Vatican passport as identification. They must relinquish their original citizenship, as the Vatican does not permit dual nationality. The perplexed expression on the face of the border policeman when presented with a Vatican passport (which looks very much like an Italian passport) is a sight to see. He turns it over and over and examines it carefully, then turns for help to his superior, who also knows nothing better than to compare the passport photo with the traveler's face and would like to pass the matter on (if only the people in line behind the barrier did not start honking impatiently...). Hardly any other passport is presented as seldomly as a Vatican passport. Even the

D. GASPARVS DE SILINON • LVC. CENTVMVIR
PRIMVS CVST. CAPITANEVS A° 1505 • OCCISVS APVD ARIMINVM R 1512

The first commander of the Swiss Guards, D. Gasparus de Silinon (1506–1512).

Vatican diplomatic corps — the nuncios and employees of the nunciatures — prefer to carry a diplomatic passport.

It is obvious that Vatican citizenship does not include the notion of nationality; you can be born a Vatican citizen (if a father already has this status, his son retains citizenship until he is twenty-five, his daughter until she marries), although you usually only receive Vatican citizenship when you have a job requiring it. As soon as the task is fulfilled, your original citizenship is immediately reinstated (at least, this is true for most persons). Lay persons having Vatican citizenship comprise the special representative of the papal state committee of the Vatican, the director of the Osservatore Romano, the papal attachés, the commander of the guard and some assistants directly responsible to the pope.

The Vatican's political system unites individuality and contradiction, anachronism and utopia in a unique way. In no other country of the world are there so many armed citizens as here, relatively speaking. The ratio of "armed" to "not armed" populace is even more blatant than in military and imperialist states: about one to three. To equal this ratio, the United States would have to arm eighty million inhabitants and the Soviet Union ninety million. This comparison does not take the weapons of the guards into account. However, it must be kept in mind that there is one policeman to protect every three Vatican citizens. Vatican City is thus not only the best guarded state, but also comes close to being a police state — a designation that is only inappropriate inasmuch as the prisons of this country are always empty. Even drivers who exceed the stipulated maximum speed limit of thirty kilometers per hour (as most do) rarely are ticketed.

At any rate, the arms of the Vatican army — sabers and halberds — are more than out of date. Hardly anyone knows that cannon are also set up here, and even fewer outsiders are aware that one of these cannon, hidden from the visitor's view by the "torre die Giovanni XXIII," is located next to the helicopter landing field and is aimed directly at Monte Mario, a strategically important (Italian) position. The remaining weapons are probably stored in the arsenal of the Swiss Guard.

Despite the fact that the Vatican has the largest proportion of armed citizens in comparison to other countries, it must not be forgotten that after the Council, Paul VI declared his willingness to radical and unilateral disarmament. Furthermore, the guard of honor, "Guardie Nobili," which had been created at the beginning of the nineteenth century from Roman nobility to replace the lancers

Commander of the Swiss Guards (left) and patrol (right) in full-dress uniform. Painting from around 1880.

and the light cavalry, who escorted the pope from the minute he left his chambers, has since been disbanded. The "Guardia Palatina di Onore," a guard of honor founded by Pius IX for diplomatic visitors and the reception rooms, has also been dissolved. The "Gendarmeria Pontifica" was formed under the original name of "Carabinieri Pontifici" in 1816 when the state was re-established by the Vienna Congress, which redrew the borders after the turbulences of the Napoleonic period. The Gendarmeria Pontifica existed in its initial state until the time of Paul VI. Its uniforms looked like a mixture of all uniforms worn during Napoleon's reign: a tall Hungarian "kolpak," above-knee boots of white leather, gilded epaulettes and a huge saber. Today its officers wear a plain uniform, like the city police in Rome, and are only responsible for keeping order. Their traditional name has, however, been retained and they are still called "gendarmi" instead of "vigili."

Of the numerous armed corps in the Vatican, only the papal Swiss Guard ("Guardia Svizzera Pontifica") has remained unaltered. It is the oldest corps, founded in 1505, and even before then, Sixtus IV had had Swiss militiamen in his service. But it was his successor, unruly Julius II, who made a real troop of them and determined their number, order of rank and duties. The flag to which the young recruits swear allegiance thus still bears Julius's coat of arms. As it turned out, Julius II's choice proved fortuitous. Twenty years afterwards the Swiss Guard demonstrated its absolute loyalty to the pope as his personal bodyguard when it defended the gates of the Vatican to cover his retreat to Castel S. Angelo on May 6, 1527. The guards let themselves literally be hacked to pieces by the advancing mercenaries. One hundred forty-seven men fell in front of the gates and forty-two locked themselves into the fortress with the pope. After the commander had personally satisfied himself that the pope was in safety, he returned to his men and died with them.

After the pope, the Swiss Guard is probably the most frequently photographed attraction. In their beautiful uniforms, they belong to the folklore image of the Vatican. Each year on the afternoon of May 6, the Guardia Svizzera Pontifica solemnly commemorates the battle in San Damaso memorial court. The ceremony ends with the swearing-in of the new recruits. With his right hand raised, three fingers spread as a symbol of the Trinity, and the left hand touching a flag lowered by a member of the Guard, each new Guard utters the following oath in his native tongue: "I swear to uphold in loyalty and faith what has been read here. May God and the Saints protect me." The recruits do not repeat the actual oath, which is read aloud as it was centuries ago when soldiers, as a rule, were illiterate. The Swiss Guard is greatly appreciated and with good reason very proud of its traditions. Of all the countries in the world, Switzerland is the only one that still pledges this honor to the pope. The old, retired members of the Guard have always taken it upon themselves to care for and preserve the uniforms that Michelangelo is supposed to have designed.

The Vatican is an absolute monarchy and at the same time the most socialistic state of the world. No citizen is allowed to possess land and real estate. This even applies to nails in the walls of an apartment and to the shutters on the windows. Usually, the interior furnishings are also state-owned. The chairs, refrigerator and mattresses in this author's apartment belonged to the state. Equal treatment is strictly observed, with respect to both allocations and wages and salaries. The largest difference between salaries never exceeds a ratio of one to three; in other words, a top salary is never as much as three times higher than the lowest basic wage. The earnings of the Cardinal Secretary of State are less than those of his chauffeur when overtime is included, because there is no provision for overtime pay for those holding executive positions. Thus, the editors-in-chief at the Osservatore Romano are paid a salary which often does not even amount to half of what the ushers receive. Absolute monarchy and real socialism, at times with a demagogic face.

A few years ago, the wages for different types of manual laborers were adjusted to correspond to Italian wages. They are now only slightly lower than the other Vatican salaries, but the extremely complicated administration made such a fuss about the matter that in the end no one was satisfied (proof that, in this instance, theorizing about socialism is an excellent pastime, but practicing it is anything but pleasant). Italian citizens employed by the Vatican do, however, have one advantage: they do not have to pay taxes, because they work in a "foreign country."

Since 1980 there has been an association of lay people employed in the Vatican that could be described as a classic trade union, even though the authorities did not want to allow that name. Some think the union was only permitted because, after all, not all forms of co-determination can be forbidden, even in a state that produces no goods whatsoever. The association had a Marxist union

Opposite: *View of the Vatican Gardens with a statue of St. Peter and Fontana dell'Aquilone (the Fountain of the Eagle) made by Vasanzio (1550-1621). The fountain's name derives from a reference to Paul V's coat of arms. The second fountain, named Sacrament Fountain, is also Vasanzio's work.*

Overleaf: *View of the Vatican Gardens from the dome of St. Peter's. In the foreground, Pope Leo XIII's coat of arms from 1880. In the Garden, the Gardener's House can be seen. It was incorporated into the remains of a medieval watch tower that probably belonged to Pope Innocent III's enclosing walls. The Administration of Archaeological Studies and Research, founded by Pope John XXIII in 1960, is located here. In the circle stands a statue of St. Peter created by Filippo Guaccarini. In the background on the right, Pope Pius IV's small house.*

The pictures of this double-spread: Pope Pius IV had this house built by Pirro Ligorio. It is comprised of a villa with a loggia and an enchanting inner courtyard. Today, the papal Academy of Sciences is housed here. The facade of the villa is adorned with beautiful stucco work by Rocco di Montefiascone.

Fountains in the Vatican Gardens: on the hill to the right next to Santo Stefano (above); the rather strangely shaped Fountain of the Eagle (far left); and the Putti Fountain in the large garden in front of the old tower in Nicholas V's enclosing wall.

Opposite: Fontana della Galera, the Galley Fountain, built according to a design by Carlo Maderno (1556-1629). The fountain portrays a leaden galley out of which water flows.

Overleaf: Palazzo del Governatorato (Government Palace). It was built by Luca Beltrami from 1928 to 1931 and was intended for use by the small papal seminar.

135

Above and opposite: *Putting a train together on the bridge over Via Gregorio VII and a railway car waiting to enter Vatican City. The Vatican railway transports only goods. The train station in the Vatican, constructed by C. Momo in 1930 under Pope Pius XI, is linked to the Italian railroad network.*

Right: *Radio Vatican is located in Nicholas V's palace and tower. The production department and studios are on Piazza Pia. The Radio Vatican transmitters, some of the most powerful in the world, are located in Santa Maria di Galeria. They were dedicated by Pope Pius XII on February 27, 1957.*

139

Facade of the church of San Giovanni in Laterano, a masterpiece designed by Alessandro Galilei. It has 15 7-meter-high statues. The church was founded by Pope Melchiades (311-314) on the site of Plautius Laternus, which Emperor Constantine had given the pope together with the Equites Sigulares barracks.

Right: *Facade of the Lateran Palace. It is located at the ancient seat of the patriarch and was the papal residence from the time of Constantine until the Avignon period (1305). The Lateran Palace was built by Domenico Fontana in 1586. The Italian Government and the Vatican signed the Lateran Treaty here on February 11, 1929.*

Opposite: *Side door of the Palazzo di Propaganda Fide, built in 1662 by Borromini, who was Bernini's successor. Pope Urban VIII had commissioned the building. Visitors can view the "Chiesa dei Re Magi" (the Church of the Three Magi) – a light, white room with wide niches along the sides – also constructed by Borromini (1666).*

141

Opposite: *The Lateran Basilica is 130 meters long and has a beautiful marble floor typical of the Latium area. The faithful were able to view the church for the first time, after its renovation by Bernini under Pope Innocent X, on the occasion of the 1650 holy year.*

Above right: *The magnificent ceiling in the left transept was designed by Taddeo Landini in 1592.*

Right: *The high tabernacle with pointed arches was created by Giovanni di Stefano from Sienna during the pontificate of Pope Urban V. Charles V of France contributed to the tabernacle. Relics of the heads of the Apostles Peter and Paul are kept in its upper part.*

Left: *The Lateran Basilica. Only the pope is allowed to say Mass at the high altar. The grave of Pope Martin V is located inside the enclosure, and two-and-a-half meters below the alter. Simone Ghini made the gravestone in 1443.*

Below left: *The marble tomb of Pietro di Piperno, a cardinal from Santa Maria Nova, is located in the fifth chapel of the left aisle and dates from 1275. Three eucharistic miracles are attributed to the cardinal.*

Above: *A statue of Emperor Constantine stands in the entrance. It comes from the springs named for him on Quirinal Hill.*

Opposite: *Interior view of Scala Sancta ("sancta sanctorum") which Pope Sixtus V had built by Domenico Fontana (1585-1590). The stairway consists of 28 marble steps and is to be ascended on one's knees. The Chapel of San Lorenzo is at the top of the stairs; it contains many relics and dates from the time of Emperor Constantine.*

The Basilica of St. Paul Outside the Wall. The cloister was begun under Abbot Pietro II da Capua at the beginning of the 12th century and completed in 1213 under Abbot Giovanni. It is Vasselletto's work.

Left: Statue of Pope Bonifacius IX (1389-1404) in the cloister. Many architectural remnants from the ancient basilica and the Roman-Christian cemetery are kept here.

Opposite: Statue of St. Paul made by Giuseppe Obici in the 19th century and mosaics of the saint executed according to a design by Filippo Agricola and Nicola Consoni. Sao Paolo Basilica is the second largest church, after St. Peter's. Its ground plan and dimensions are almost identical to the Basilica of Ulpia on Foro Traiano. The church was badly damaged by a fire during the night of July 15, 1823.

Opposite and above: *The basilica of Santa Maria Maggiore, or Saint Maria of the Snow. Domenico Fontana began construction of this church in 1585 for Pope Sixtus V.* Above: *Allessandro Fuga's high altar.*

Ferdinando Fuga constructed the facade of Santa Maria Maggiore from 1743 to 1750 and accentuated it with numerous sculptures. The Romanesque bell tower dating from 1377 is the highest in Rome.

Below: *A ceremony on the splendid stairs of the apse. The stairway, also called Liberiana, was probably built by Pope Liberius. Pope Sixtus III had the present basilica of Santa Maria Maggiore erected immediately after the Council of Ephesus in 431. Pope Clement X commissioned Carlo Rinaldi to build the apse in 1673.*

Above: *The "Hall of the Swiss Guards" in the papal residence at Castel Gandolfo, in a linear arrangement with a papal throne. The pope uses the Hall for audiences with the faithful, especially in summer.*

Opposite: *The Holy See proclaimed Castel Gandolfo to be entailed property in 1604. It became the papal summer residence, especially after Pope Urban VIII had the villa built for the Popes' summer stay in 1624. Twenty-eight popes have resided here up to the present. The interior is impressive: the Hall of the Swiss, the Hall of the Grooms, the Hall of the Noble Guard, the Throne Room, the papal chapel, the Gallery of Pope Benedict XIV, and Pope Clement XIV's Dining Hall. A terrace and the outer wall of Domitian's covered walkway are located in the spacious garden of the papal villa.*

member draw up its statutes and articles. It also immediately made radical demands reminiscent of a policy of sovietism. Strikes and demonstrations were threatened in heated meetings, which was just what the press was waiting for. They looked forward eagerly to the unheard-of, very first strike in the Vatican. However, the Vatican also has a bit of concrete communism in the respect that there may be a union, but there are no strikes.

In reality, the Vatican city-state is not just an absolute monarchy, but a theocracy, because its head of state is the vicar of Christ on earth and the head of the Church. He is pope and king according to God's will, even if he is elected by his fellow cardinals. The cardinals, his advisors and adjutants, have the status of "princes" and "archdukes." The "papal yearbook" indicates that the Lord also provides the legal foundation and his will is law: "John Paul II, bishop of Rome, vicar of Jesus Christ, successor of the prince of Apostles, supreme pontiff of the universal church, patriarch of the west, primate of Italy, archbishop and metropolitan of the Roman province, sovereign of the state of Vatican City, servant of the servants of God."

John Paul I was the first to dispense with the coronation, a ceremony in which the tiara was set on the pope's head as a symbol of superiority over all earthly power. This ritual was replaced by the ceremony of the "solemn beginning of sanctification" from which all mention of secular rule has been removed. Secular power today is limited solely to an area of 44 hectares (17,8 acres) and 350 inhabitants. The tiara is a last emblem from the history of the "frog" ("ranocchia"), as the papal coat of arms is familiarly called in Vatican colloquial speech (and as a matter of fact, its outlines are faintly reminiscent of a frog). When Pope Woityla ordered his coat of arms, he upset the heraldist with the nonchalant remark that the latter could draw what he pleased provided that the Cross as the sign of Christ and the letter "M" as a sign of veneration for the Mother of God were included. The prelate was supposedly thunderstruck. He adhered to his claim that the use of letters in a coat of arms almost amounted to heresy and was an impropriety that completely disregarded all the rules of the art of heraldry. John Paul II is said to have answered: "Do as you like, but the "M" has to stay." The heraldry specialist, a friendly Anglo-Saxon prelate who had already designed hundreds of coats of arms for bishops, swallowed and remained silent. After all, he could not very well resign from office.

Opposite: *The papal throne of Innocent X, elected pope in 1644, is housed in the papal villa of Castel Gandolfo.*

VIII – PAPAL AUTHORITY,
THE VATICAN'S ROLE IN THE WORLD

*Pope Pius VII returning to Rome from France in
a horse-drawn carriage. Numerous horse-drawn
coaches once belonging to popes and cardinals are
on display in the historical museum Pope Paul VI
had built under the so-called Square Garden. The
museum was opened to the public in 1973.*

*T*he pope has great authority within the Church. He embodies a mandate subordinate solely to divine law that also entails complete servitude: he is "servant of the servants of God". Furthermore, "the pope is the successor of St. Peter and is endowed not merely with a primacy of honor, but with supreme and complete powers of jurisdiction; not only in matters of faith and morals, but also concerning discipline and rule over the Church throughout the world".

The significance of the papacy as a spiritual presence and motivation for the search for peace, justice and humanity in our time has led to the people's great respect for the pope. Through the centuries many, from Eutiche to Vozzio and Martin Luther, from Henry VIII to Joseph II, have repeatedly, and sometimes very strongly, questioned papal authority. The history of the Church is, therefore, also a history of secessions, schisms and ruptures induced by theological disputes. The real reasons for most, however, were politics justified by theological differences. The divisions between the Christian denominations that have resulted are a source of bitterness for the successors of Christ. To overcome and reunite what history has divided, an ecumenical dialogue has been started in the twentieth century. It was given a great boost by Paul VI, who apologized for the Catholic Church's part in these long-standing divisions.

Even though he feels the nearness of all Catholics, the pope is the loneliest of people, because he is responsible only to God for his decisions, notwithstanding the fact that he listens to the advice of the bishops and cardinals. And as God's emissary, the pope's often unpopular decisions can affect the lives of believers deeply, often dramatically. Just consider the demands the Church places on family life and reproduction, demands that deviate so sharply from contemporary customs and attitudes. In contrast to common and polemic conceptions, and even to the usual picture people have about the pope's life, (hence, the expression "to live like the pope"), within the Vatican talk of the pope's duties and of his heavy daily burden — a burden which sometimes cannot be borne for long — is more realistic. On the occasion of John Paul I's death, a picture which could hardly have been more descriptive and characteristic was published in a famous French weekly depicting the pope being crushed by the tiara.

The pope relies on the Secretariat of State in governmental matters. The history of this institution will not be dealt with here, except to say that Paul VI more clearly defined its tasks in the Apostolic

Constitution "Regimini Ecclesiae" (published on August 15, 1967) when the Curia was reformed. The main task of the Secretariat of State is "to aid and support the pope in his concern for the entire Church as well as in the relations to the departments of the Roman Curia." In reality, the Secretariat of State carries out a broad range of activities, since its function "is to fulfill all tasks assigned by the pope."

The Secretary of State is the head of the Secretariat of State and usually a cardinal (if not, he bears the title "pro-segretario"). Next to the pope, he is the highest authority in the Vatican and the pope's prime coworker and advisor. A substitute (a bishop) for the Secretary of State assists the Cardinal Secretary of State, his direct superior. In addition, the substitute has numerous direct contacts to the pope. The chief assistant to the substitute is an assessor. Over one hundred priests (almost all of whom bear the title "Monsignore") work in the Secretariat and come from the administration and diplomatic branches (the latter have their own "Accademia"). However, some lay people and nuns also work there.

The Council for the Public Affairs of the Church is led by a secretary (a bishop) subordinate to the Cardinal Secretary of State. He is responsible for relations with the governments of the different countries of the world and deals with the problems arising in various countries in the relationship between Church and state. Each Monsignore who works in the Secretariat of State and the Council for the Public Affairs of the Church is responsible for one or more countries (usually according to language). One of a monsignore's duties is, naturally, to provide the pope with important documents and reports from his respective countries and to prepare the speeches the pope gives when he receives bishops and diplomats. When the pope travels, the appropriate "specialists" for the countries to be visited are members of his "entourage".

As a sovereign state, the Holy See accredits and receives ambassadors. At the present, the diplomatic corps accredited by the Holy See comprises about 110 countries and legations. Not included are representatives of the socialist countries from the East Bloc, with the exception of Yugoslavia, whereas many African and Latin American countries with Communist governments are represented by consuls. Recently, the consulate of the United States which had only supported a personal representative of the President at the Holy See was opened (or rather, reopened). In its turn, the Vatican established a nunciature in Washington. The Council for the Public Affairs of the Church, which corresponds approximately to the Ministry of Foreign Affairs in a state government, coordinates the activities of such nunciatures.

The diplomatic representatives of the Holy See are bishops, who bear the title "nuncio" if they are also recognized as deans (according to the provisions of the 1815 Vienna Congress ratified in Vienna in 1861). If this recognition is withheld, the representative is called a "pro-nuncio," but of course he performs the same functions as a full nuncio. A nuncio often heads several nunciatures for financial and personnel reasons (as seen in Latin America and Africa). The nunciatures require a minimum of organization and employ only a few persons in addition to the nuncio: one or two Monsignori who act as deputy for the public affairs of the Church and as secretary. In rare cases, a chauffeur who also serves as gardener and caretaker is employed.

The establishment of diplomatic relations is an abiding concern of the Holy See; not only in order to protect Church rights and freedom of religion, but also to serve the cause of peace. Countries that for decades have no longer recognized the Vatican are listed in the Papal Yearbook "Annuario Pontificio", as are some states no longer in existence since 1945 (e.g. Latvia and Estonia). The Holy See is never the first party to sever diplomatic relations. The seat of Taipei (Formosa) is still listed under the entry for China in the "Annuario," although only a deputy for public affairs, and not a nuncio is named. A break with the remnants of old China is not desired, but the possibility of future relations to large Communist China is also not to be excluded. The Vatican is a master of legal and diplomatic delicacy, and its patience extends back for centuries.

Sometimes – very rarely – the diplomacy of the Holy See transcends the discreet and secretive role it normally assumes in solving problems between nations. It then acts openly as a mediator, for example, in the solution of the difficult Beagle Canal conflict between the two "Catholic" countries Chile and Argentina.

Due to the Holy See's dedication to peace, the furthering of humanity, and justice and equality among the peoples of the earth, it has observers, representatives and delegates in international institutions such as the UN (without the right to vote, of course), UNESCO, FAO, the Council of Europe, the EC, the organizations of American countries and the World Organization for Tourism. Proof of interest in these organizations is evident from the papal visits of the last decades, including Paul VI's and John Paul II's visits to the UN, to mention just two. Paul II demonstrated by his visit to the UN that he was an "expert for humanity," because he advocated the cause of peace for everyone.

Lay persons are prone to confusing the Vatican and the state of Vatican City with the Holy See. The state is a civic organization that possesses real estate and has its own structures, whereas the Holy See is the seat of the pope and papal government for the entire Church. One part of this government, the Secretariat of State, is mentioned above with its Department of Internal Affairs (headed by the substitute) and the Department of Foreign Affairs (headed by the Secretary for Foreign Affairs). On the other hand, the difference between the Vatican and the Holy See should not be overemphasized since the Vatican really represents only the small amount of land and "worldly power" necessary for the universal soul of the Church to retain its human and historical personification and its full freedom. This point must be made so that the Church is not seen as a curious, historical phenomenon — a wonderful sort of antique — which you only need to know about because of its cultural richness and incomparable treasures. Were this the case, the Vatican would be a huge museum with the folkloric traits of a religious denomination. For the same reason, it should be remembered that the external organization of the Church, which converges in this small state, was cut down in size due by historical events and is now squeezed into the city of Rome.

The pope rules "collectively" with the "brothers of the episcopate" and they, the bishops, head the divisions of the Church, the dioceses, "collectively with the pope." In addition to the pope, there is also the "Sacred College of Cardinals." During the first centuries of the Church's existence, the cardinals merely held leading positions in the various Roman "parishes" and were the deacons and bishops of the cities in the area around Rome. They were all advisors of the Bishop of Rome, the pope. Up to the last century, the cardinals were not always bishops, nor even priests, as "cardinal" was an honorary title. Johannes XXIII was the first to decree that all cardinals had to be bishops.

Pope Pius XI (1922–1939) on a lithograph produced for the 1925 holy year. The treaty between the Holy See and Italy was signed under Pius XI on February 11, 1929, in the Lateran Basilica. Pius XI was also the first pope to address the "Qui arcano Dei" encyclical to the whole world via radio on February 12, 1931.

Paul VI specified in addition that they had to hand in their resignation from Curial activities on completion of their seventy-fifth year of life and that they were not allowed to participate in the conclave, which elects the pope, after their eightieth birthday. This regulation has been a source of controversy up to the present, for, it is said, if the pope can exercise his office until his death, it is incomprehensible that cardinals, who occupy much less important positions, should not be allowed to do the same.

If the pope is comparable to a monarch, the cardinals are princes and also have a right to the title "Eminence." Even if they live outside the Vatican, they are considered its citizens. Some of them, called "residenziali," head a diocese, whereas others lead the institutions and departments of the Curia and the organs of the Vatican. They assist the pope in Church government, particularly by heading the congregations and other organs in the various areas of Church work. Each cardinal is appointed by the pope for a five-year period. All appointments become invalid when the pope dies and must be reconfirmed by the next pontiff elected.

A cardinal who heads a congregation bears the title "prefect." His main assistants are a secretary (a bishop) and an under-secretary, both of whom are appointed by the pope. The work of each congregation is supported by a type of council comprised of cardinals and diocesan bishops, as well as a certain number of priests and laity also elected for five years. The "Annuario" describes the congregations as follows: "They are standing committees of cardinals that deal with the affairs of the Church. The congregations are comprised of cardinals, of whom one holds the position of prefect. Each congregation's range of activities is determined by the various branches of the administration, even though the Church makes no formal distinction between the legislative and administrative branches. The congregations are generally limited according to territory..."

Paul III (1534 – 1549) established the Congregation for the Doctrine of the Faith under the name of the Sacred Congregation of the Universal Inquisition, the purpose of which was to defend the integrity of the faith from heresy. It was generally known as "Sant' Ufficio" throughout the centuries and had a bad, at times ominous, reputation. In 1965, Paul VI changed its name and functions according to the spirit of the reforms resulting from the Council. The "Motu Proprio," which established the Congregation specifies some of its responsibilities: "questions concerning the doctrine of the faith and morals, and matters concerning beliefs; examination of new doctrines and support of studies and congresses applying to these doctrines, the rejection of teachings that contradict the principles of the faith; the examination and perhaps condemnation of books; "privilegium fide"; the condemnation of transgressions against the faith."

The Congregation probably carries out the most delicate task, which at the same time is the one most closely integrated into the Catholic Church. The Congregation must not only bear the burden of memories of the past, but also of the necessity to make decisions which can be far-reaching. An international theological commission is affiliated with this Congregation and supposed to assist in the examination of doctrinal questions by means of scholastic authority; it consists of theologians of different nationalities and different schools who are "marked by learning and loyalty." Members of the commission are appointed by the pope and never number more than thirty. The Catholic Church's strictness in matters of doctrine is well known; however, it is generally also true that the leadership of agencies of this sort is entrusted to extremely capable people. Joseph Ratzinger, a German theologian, is presently prefect of this Congregation.

The Congregation for the Bishops was founded by Sixtus V (one of the reformers and organizers of the roman Curia and the Church state) in 1588. It underwent a process of reformation at the beginning of the twentieth century until Paul VI specified its functions as "the establishment, division and unification of the dioceses, provinces and regions of the Church, as well as the inspection of borders; in addition, the establishment of vicariates and prelacies for pastoral work in various regions and for the benefit of special groups; preparations for the appointment of bishops, apostolic administrators, coadjutors and suffragans... Furthermore, the responsibilities of this Congregation also include the observation and supervision of all matters concerning the persons and offices of the bishops and the status of the dioceses, the examination of the five-year reports... to inspect everything pertaining to the conducting of sub-councils and bishops' conferences...." The Papal Commission on Pastoral Work with People, founded in 1970, and the Commission on Latin America established by Pius XII, which also incorporates a General Council for Latin America are affiliated with this Congregation.

The lay person, confronted with so many names of congregations, commissions and councils, may perhaps believe that they are actually all one and the same, in reality, however, the necessity for a well-structured organization in the Church increases constantly, corresponding to the rate at which yet unsolved problems and tasks arise. Structures which take account of the special demands of evangelization and unity are imposed on the partially secular structures of this organization. People interested in the Vatican normally fail to consider this aspect of it, yet it represents one of the basic features of the Holy See and its universality.

The Congregation for the Eastern Churches originated with an insitution established by Pius IX, the responsibilities and powers of which have changed and expanded over the course of time. It resembles the Congregation for the Bishops, but differs in its concentration on the faithful of the Eastern denominations. The approximately ten million Eastern believers are in a very difficult position, as at least half of them live in countries where freedom of religion is limited or completely abolished. The Eastern Catholic Churches include the Antiochan Church (widespread especially in Palestine, Syria and Mesopotamia, as well as in a part of Malabar), the Alexandrine Church (the Copts, Ethiopeans and Eritreans), the Byzantine (or Constantinoplean) Church, the Syrian-Oriental (or Chaldean) Church, and the Armenian Church.

The Congregation for the Sacraments and Mass was not established until 1975 by Paul VI. "It is concerned with all matters pertaining to the seven sacraments, in consideration of the authority of the Congregation for the Doctrine of the Faith in respect to doctrine, in consideration of the authority of the Supreme Tribunal of the Apostolic Signature regarding the transfer of competence in marriage hearings, as well as the responsibility to supervise the administration of justice and the establishment of regional and superregional tribunals according to law; in consideration of the authority of 'Sacra Romana Rota' in regard to marriage annulment proceedings."

The Congregation for the Clergy is rooted historically in the congregation founded in 1564 after the Council of Trent for the correct pragmatic interpretation of the norms established by the

Council itself. Paul VI changed the Congregation's name in 1967 and defined its sphere of authority, which is supervised by three different offices. The first office is responsible for the spiritual and cultural advancement of the clergy; the second, for the proclamation of the Word of God, the Apostles and the Catechism; the third, for the administration and preservation of temporal goods, i.e., the supervision of charities, churches, holy places and objects and treasures of art, and the compensation and guidance of the clergy.

The Congregation for Members of Orders and for Secular Institutes was founded in 1586. It has, of course, undergone some changes over the centuries. Today it is concerned "with all matters pertaining to the orders and congregations for men and women, as well as the communities, in respect to management, discipline, education, possessions, justice and privileges. Its authority covers all aspects of the lives of members of orders: Christian life, life in the order and Church life."

The Congregation for the Propagation of the Faith, "De Propaganda Fide," has its origins in the cardinals' commission for the missions in East and West India, for the Italo-Greeks and in general for the affairs of the Catholic Church in Protestant countries. The commission was founded by Pius V (1566 – 1572) and Gregory XIII (1572 – 1585). Today, the congregation regulates and coordinates the work and cooperation between evangelizing and missionary activities throughout the world, according to the resolutions of the Second Vatican Council. It oversees some regions in southeastern Europe, North and South America, almost all of Africa and the Far East, New Zealand, Oceania and nearly all of the Philippines. It determines "the mission areas as expedient, watches over the management of the missions and examines all questions and reports submitted by the ordinaries and the bishops' conferences, it supervises the Christian life of the faithful and clergy discipline as well as all charity associations and associations of Catholic Action, and finally is responsible for optimal work in Catholic schools, especially in the seminaries." In addition to the cardinals appointed by the pope, this Congregation includes the presidents of the Secretariats for the Unity of Christians, for Non-Believers and for Non-Christians, because these secretariats are also concerned with evangelization.

Pope Clement X (1670 – 1676) on a medal by G. L. Bernini. In the "Museo di Palazzo Venezia", Rome.

The Congregation for Beatification and Canonization Proceedings was only established recently to assume its responsibilities formerly delegated to a different congregation. It deals with very complicated and strict canonization proceedings in which all aspects of the life and faith of the person to be canonized are examined. Reviewers have to carry out investigations and then present them to the cardinals and bishops of the Congregation, although the final decision is reserved for the pope. It is said that several canonization examinations already completed, one of them concerning Pope Pius IX, have been lying on the pope's desk for years awaiting a final judgement.

The Congregation for the Catholic Education System goes back to a congregation founded by Sixtus V that supervised and regulated education at the University of Rome and elsewhere in Europe. Since the nineteenth century other bishops, starting with Leo XII and including Pius X and Benedict XV, have been interested in the teaching at seminaries and universities. Paul VI gave the congregation its present structure, and expanded and exactly defined its responsibilities, which are divided into three sectors. The first one deals with the functioning of all seminaries and educational institutions, both secular and those belonging to religious orders, from the curricula to the administration. The second sector has jurisdiction over all Catholic universities, departments, institutes and higher schools, whether they are run by lay people or members of orders. About 400 Catholic universities and 132 universities and departments of church studies scattered on all continents require supervision. In particular, this office must ensure that the study of theology at the universities is suitable for lay students. The third sector is responsible for all schools and institutions of education, regardless of how dependent they are on church authority.

The pope's administration of the Church hinges on the congregations. Each congregation has well-defined responsibilities to prevent the conflicts of authority, that are always considered a heavy risk by the Roman Curia. Nobody guards a sphere of authority as jealously as the leaders of the separate departments. It is not without importance that a cardinal, i.e., an "advisor to the pope" and a "prince," heads each congregation and is regularly received by the pope. This collegiality guarantees the unity of government within the Church hierarchy.

In addition to the congregations, a great number of other organs belong to the Curia: secretariats, councils, commissions and committees that fulfill certain responsibilities in the various sectors of Church activities. They range from purely spiritual work to scholastic and cultural activities and from ethical to historical work. In general, these organs were not founded until recently. We won't confuse the reader by listing all of the bodies, but the most important ones will be mentioned for thoroghness' sake.

The Secretariat for the Unity of Christians was founded by John XXIII and reconfirmed by Paul VI. It fulfills ecumenical responsibilities through its two departments: the Department for Relations to Eastern Christians (the Orthodox churches) and the Department for Relations to Western Christians (the Protestant churches). The ecumenical dialogue in general saw a significant upswing after the Council, although the dialogue with the Orthodox churches is much more active at the present than that with the Protestant churches.

Paul VI founded the Secretariat for Non-Christians twenty years ago to establish contacts and a dialogue with all believers. The commissions entrusted with relations to Jewry and Islam are affiliated with this institution. A third secretariat, for Non-Believers, examines atheism and certainly faces difficult partners in a dialogue.

A Papal Council for Laity deals with making the Church accessible to lay people. To promote justice and peace among people according to the "Gaudium et Spes" document from the Council, Paul VI set up the Commission "Justitia et Pax." The "Cor unum" Commission was established to further awareness of the problems of poverty and hunger in the Third World and of the search for better means of providing concrete aid. It also coordinates the different activities of the numerous Catholic charity groups. Even newer is the papal Council for Culture, which works within the Church, but also aims at cooperating with other international organizations, for example, UNESCO. A large number of the organs comprising the Roman Curia directly serve the management of the Church. The ever-present possibility of a conflict between the central administration and the periphery and between the Curia and the regional churches is expertly minimized by appointing numerous bishops as representatives on the commissions as well as counsels in the outlying areas.

Pope John XXIII. Official photograph on the occasion of his coronation as pope on October 28, 1958.

A special task of the organs is to combine centralism with local autonomy, no small fear when one considers that about 100 bishops' conferences with 2,400 dioceses exist throughout the world.

The pope's daily schedule is arranged by the prefecture for the papal household. This also applies to both his trips in Italy and abroad — which of course are also coordinated with the Secretariat of State. Under Pope John Paul II, the untiring pilgrim and systematic visitor of the Roman parishes and Italian dioceses, this prefecture has had its work cut out for it, as each audience and each public appearance has to be arranged down to the last detail. The chief difficulty of this responsibility is that the pope does not adhere to protocol or planned schedules, especially when he is among crowds of people. This breaks down the entire time schedule to the annoyance of those who have very carefully — and perhaps pedantically — undertaken the arrangements. Accompanying the pope on his trips abroad, often entails running a constant obstacle course for his co-workers: plane, helicopter, car, crowd of people, then back to the car, helicopter, and plane. It is no wonder that every once in awhile a Monsignore or two nods off during the long festivities (or, as spiteful tongues claim, while standing).

All central organs of the Church are based in Rome, where they enjoy the privileges of extraterritoriality. They are considered legally to be areas belonging to the Holy See. There is not enough room for everything in the Vatican, and in view of the growth of the Church organization, more and more extraterritorial areas will probably have to be established in the future.

The three basilicas — St. John Lateran, St. Paul's Outside the Walls and Saint Maria Maggiore — are historical and spiritual expansions of the Vatican considered the jewels of Christian Rome.

St. John Lateran, the Cathedral of Rome, rises on "Celio," one of the seven hills of Rome where, according to Tacitus, the properties of the Lateran family were located. Tradition has it that the land and buildings were a present of Emperor Constantine to the pope. The basilica has been part of the entire eventful history of the spread of Christianity in Rome. It was the seat of the popes until their return from the "Babylonian Captivity at Avignon," and the location of several ecumenical councils, including those in 1123 and in 1215.

The façade of St. John Lateran bears the inscription assigning the role of mother to the basilica: "Sacrosancta Lateranensis ecclesia omnium urbis et orbis ecclesiarum mater et caput." This idea of the dominance of the basilica goes back to the distant time of the "Donation" of Emperor Constantine. As in all four Roman basilicas, the signs of Church history can be read here. The papal palace, built by Domenico Fontana on commission of Sixtus V, adjoins the basilica. The cloister, a work of the Vassalletto family, that dates from the thirteenth century, is one of the richest, most impressive works of art in Rome. The palace, which had decayed over the centuries, has been restored and is the seat of the vicariate (i.e., the cardinal appointed by the pope as representative of the diocese of Rome).

St. Paul's Outside the Walls, also called "basilica ostiense," lies on the outskirts of town about two kilometers from the Aurelian city walls. It is written in "Liber Pontificalis" that Constantine built this basilica to create a final resting place for the mortal remains of St. Paul. Excavations in the nineteenth century proved the existence of this first basilica. Traces of adjacent Christian graves were uncovered during recent excavations. It is certain that the basilica was built in the time of Emperors Valentinian II, Theodosius, and Arcadian. An inscription made during the pontificate of Sirius (384 – 399) implies that the foundations had been completed.

Two monasteries later combined to form the Benedictine Abbey, arose near the basilica. Even today, the monastery still belongs to the Benedictine order and the abbot is invested with the rank of bishop. The unfortified basilica, the abbey and the nearby village were plundered by the Lombards in the eighth century and, along with the "urbe" (the city of Rome), were systematically pillaged by the Saracens a century later. For this reason, the entire complex was surrounded by a wall in the ninth century. The basilica contained glorious works of art until a fire destroyed the nave and the ceiling in 1823. The "confessio" and the tabernacle by Arnolfo da Cambio, a part of the transept and the apse with Venetian mosaics dating from the twelfth and thirteenth centuries, were saved. The basilica was rebuilt according to the design of the antique basilica. The cloister, decorated by the same artists who worked in St. John Lateran, possesses a special religious significance expressed by Pietro da Capua in the following verse: "The army of monks reads, studies and prays here (and because it includes those who have chosen a monastical life, it is called 'Chiostro') it is sealed and rejoices with Christ in the pious flock of monks."

A delightful legend recorded by Brother Bartolomeo da Trento and portrayed in the basilica's mosaics explains why Santa Maria Maggiore was erected on its site. Pope Liberius and a wealthy patrician wished to build a place of worship in honor of the Virgin, but could not decide where. Both dreamed during the same night, on August 5, 352, that it had snowed on Esquilin Hill (in Rome, it usually does not snow, even in winter). When they awoke, they saw that their dreams had come true and the hill was white with snow. Thus they built the basilica, which bears many names, among them "Santa Maria della neve" (St. Maria of the Snow), on this site.

Since the beginnings of Christianity, the cult of the Virgin has been widespread in Rome, and as late as the nineteenth century there were approximately 1,500 chapels and tabernacles dedicated to the Madonna. In reference to its primacy among all other churches in Rome dedicated to the Virgin, this basilica was eventually named "Santa Maria Maggiore." The present basilica, built by Pope Sixtus III (432 – 440) is not identical with the one erected by Pope Liberius. However, the basilica is certainly one of the oldest, most honorable churches as well as a glorification of the dogma of the Madonna's motherhood as defined by the Council of Ephesus: Maria is not only the "Mother of Christ," but also the "Mother of God" ("teotokos"). Like all great buildings, this basilica also underwent several alterations in the course of time, the most important being the addition of a second façade (on the sides of the apse) near the end of the seventeenth century.

The list of works about the Vatican, the Holy See and the Roman Curia is virtually endless. Interest in them has been awakened again and again, from generation to generation. There is a saying among journalists that "il Vaticano fa notizia" ("news from the Vatican is always popular"). But when news is lacking, it is simply made up and no doubt supported by the thick wall of silence surrounding life in the Curia. This silence leads to the temptation to spread suppositions and fantastic implications.

Although a tiny state the Vatican has a strong aura of magic. As soon as the magic is overcome, it becomes apparent that it is also a very concrete phenomenon with human aspects, a bureaucracy and an organizational structure. It is therefore possible to observe and describe it from various angles. Nevertheless, an air of "secrecy" that can be called forth at will — even if there is no reason for it — envelops the Vatican. Everything is possible, and some people, perhaps influenced by reading trivial literature during their youth, have even told of murders by poison. Others have described all the species of birds living within the four hundred hectares of the Vatican, from the falcon on the dome to the raven in the Gardens. Still others have written about the wildflowers.

These are just more examples of how at the Vatican the sublime manifests next to the commonplace, and holiness next to profanity. They are often so entwined that it is impossible to recognize where one ends and the other begins. The old and the new blend in a like matter. Here, you live with timeless works of art, even as you participate in the course of history. Alongside the masterpieces and the spirituality that this state represents live the people who go shopping in the "Annona" (duty-free grocery store). The soldier from the Swiss Guards dressed in his elegant uniform stands next to a laborer in his work clothes, and nobody is disturbed except the tourists, who stop astonished at "Porta S. Anna," blocking traffic. Maybe it is the visitors who remind the people used to life here of the extraordinariness of the Vatican. Sometimes the sensitivity of a poet is required to penetrate the mysteriousness, or to at least approach it, and to show its unique beauty.

Tano Citeroni has succeeded in doing so. What I have written is only the background for his magnificent photographs. I have tried to portray the story and the history, daily life and the everlasting, in a narrative without clichés and, above all, without being trite or repeating well-known anecdotes. If I have not been successful, I beg the reader's pardon. As compensation, you can enjoy the beautiful pictures.

Opposite: *Entrance to the Vatican Museums. Until 1932, the only way to gain access to the Museums was through the Palazzo Apostolico or the Vatican Gardens. Pope Pius XI had Giuseppe Monno build a separate door into the 18th-century fortified Vatican walls. The statues are of Michelangelo and Raphael.*

The spiral stairs to the Vatican Museums. The stairway has up and down ramps and, designed by Giuseppe Monno, rises 16 meters over a length of 98 meters. A Maraini made the bronze railing with the papal coat of arms. Visitors who do not care to climb the stairs to the Museums can travel in comfort by elevator.

Opposite: *Cortile della Pigna, the Courtyard of the Pigna, is the northern part of Bramante's Courtyard of the Belvedere. The court is dominated by the impressive niche named for Bramante, although it was really constructed by Pirro Ligorio in 1500. The Courtyard owes its name to a huge bronze pinecone from Roman times found near Agrippa Springs. It originally was used to adorn a fountain near the Temple of Isis.*

Above: *Cortile della Pigna, the Courtyard of the Pigna, extends for a length of about 300 meters between the small palace of Pope Innocent VIII in the north and the Palazzo Pontificio, the Papal Palace, in the south.*

Left: *The courtyard that leads from the entrance to the Vatican Gallery of Paintings and the Simonetti Stairway.*

Opposite: *The famous statue of Apollo in the Courtyard of the Belvedere is attributed to Leochares. It was probably discovered in Anzio near the end of the 15th century and belonged to Pope Julius II before he was elected pope. The statue became particularly famous in the Neo-Classical era, because Winckelmann considered it to be the personification of ideal beauty.*

View of the Courtyard of the Belvedere, designed by Giacomo di Pietrasante. Pope Clement XIV had the garden, which Pope Julius II originally had designed as a rectangle, altered by Dori and Simonetti to an octagonal shape between 1771 and 1772. One of the most famous statues exhibited here is the Laocoön Group.

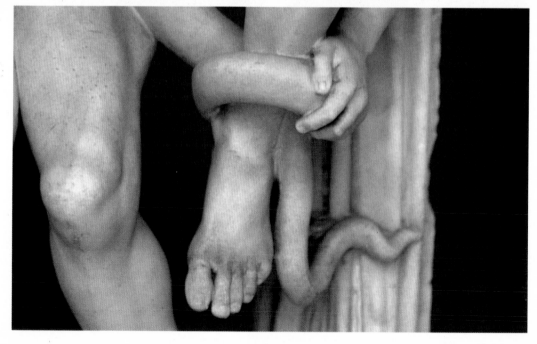

The Laocoön Group was created by the sculptors Rodi Hagasandros, Athanodoros and Polydoros. It was discovered in Seven Halls on Esquilin Hill on January 14, 1505.

The Greek group is an unusually expressive representation of the mythological figure of Laocoön, a priest of the Thymbraic Apollo, who died with his sons when he was attacked by two huge serpents. This sculpture had a considerable influence on the artists of the 16th century, starting with Michelangelo.

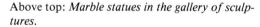

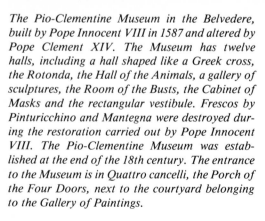

The Pio-Clementine Museum in the Belvedere, built by Pope Innocent VIII in 1587 and altered by Pope Clement XIV. The Museum has twelve halls, including a hall shaped like a Greek cross, the Rotonda, the Hall of the Animals, a gallery of sculptures, the Room of the Busts, the Cabinet of Masks and the rectangular vestibule. Frescos by Pinturicchino and Mantegna were destroyed during the restoration carried out by Pope Innocent VIII. The Pio-Clementine Museum was established at the end of the 18th century. The entrance to the Museum is in Quattro cancelli, the Porch of the Four Doors, next to the courtyard belonging to the Gallery of Paintings.

Above top: *Marble statues in the gallery of sculptures.*

Above: *Busts including those of Emperor Caracalla, Marcus Aurelius, Hadrian, Troian, Nero as well as the Kitharodiaos Apollo and a youthful Octavian are found in the Gallery of Busts.*

Above right: *The Three Graces, a Roman copy of the Greek original.*

Right and opposite: *Important works are displayed in the Gallery of Statues: for example, the Amazon from Villa Mattei, the reposing satyr, the sleeping Ariane, and a portrayal of Poseidippos, a comic playwright who lived in the 3rd century BC.*

176

The Gallery of Busts is comprised of three rooms.
A statue of Jupiter seated is especially interesting,
as are those of Hercules, Saturn, Menelaos,
Serapion, Antinoos, a woman with a mask and
the head of a warrior.

Left and opposite: *The Gallery of Statues used to
be an uncovered loggia in Belvedere Palace. Jacopo di Pietrasanta built the palace according to a
design by Antonio Pollaiolo. Under Pope Clement XIV (1769-1774) it was changed to a sculpture gallery. Pope Pius VI had it enlarged and
connected to the Hall of the Animals in 1776.*

Young admirer in the Stanza di Eliodoro (the Room of Heliodoros), painted by Raphael in 1514. The painting refers to Julius II's crusade against foreigners in Italy and to the pope's victory over the enemies of the church.

Right: Detail from Raphael's loggias. Giovanni da Udine executed the stucco work. The vault, lunettes, pillars and pilaster strips are richly decorated with fantastic paintings: flowers, fruits, mythological figures, festoons and garlands. These motifs go back to the adornments found during the excavations of the ancient rooms called the "Grottos;" this type of adornment was, therefore, named "grotesque."

Opposite: Raphael built the loggias from 1512 to 1518. The floor was covered with majolica tiles from the Della Robbia family's workshop (1518); they were replaced in 1869, as they had worn down. The loggias extend for thirteen spans with vaults and pavilions. The first twelve spans are decorated with Old Testament scenes in four sections, whereas scenes from the New Testament are represented in the last one. There is a total of fifty-two Bible episodes.

Opposite: *The discus thrower, one of the most famous copies of Myron's original. It stands in Biga Hall in the Chiaromonti Gallery, which Caporese built for Pope Pius VI.*

Above top: *Madonna with child and angels by Giotto (1266-1337) in the painting gallery of the Musei Galleria Pontefice.*

Above: *St. Nicholas of Bari saves a sailing-ship from being wrecked. By Fra Angelico (1387-1455), in the painting gallery in the Musei Galleria Pontefice.*

Overleaf: *The architecture and frescoes of the Sala Regia, begun by Antonio da Sangallo the Younger in 1546 during the pontificate of Paul III. The Sala Regia was originally used to receive rulers. The doors open onto the Pauline Chapel, the Sistine Chapel and the Sala Ducale, which can be seen in this picture.*

ENTIS VICTO CAPTOQVE FRIDERICVS PAS...A SVBLI... IMPERAT ...ET ...VON
...ICITVR ITA PONTIFICI SVA DIGNITAS VENETAE REIPVBLICAE VENETIIS SECVR...

Raphael's small loggia is located in the Segretaria di Stato (Secretariat of State) building and is used as a waiting room. Raphael and his school created this work on commission of Pope Leo X for secretary, Cardinal Bibbiena.

Right: *The Hall of Imitations in the Museo Gregoriano Egizio, established by Pope Gregory XVI in 1839. Reproductions of Egyptian art by Roman artists from the 2nd and the 3rd centuries are exhibited here. Most of the works are from Hadrian's villa in Tivoli.*

Opposite: *The Gallery of Maps, which Pope Gregory XIII had built as the third floor in the west wing of the Corridoio di Belvedere. Maschinero was the architect, Muziano and Nebbia decorated the vault and the Dominican researcher Ignazio Danti painted the imposing maps.*

186

PIVS·IX·PONT·MAX·
LATERITIO·PAVIMENTO
MARMOREVM·SVBSTITVIT
PONT·AN·XXXII·

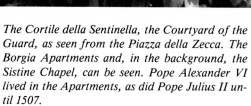

The Cortile della Sentinella, the Courtyard of the Guard, as seen from the Piazza della Zecca. The Borgia Apartments and, in the background, the Sistine Chapel, can be seen. Pope Alexander VI lived in the Apartments, as did Pope Julius II until 1507.

Above and opposite: *The Sistine chapel is one of the main attractions in the Vatican Palaces. It was built by Giovanni dei Dolci on commission of Pope Sixtus IV and decorated by the great painters of the Umbrian and Florentine Schools - including Pinturicchio, Perugino, Ghirlandario, Botticelli and Signorelli. Later, Pope Julius commissioned Michelangelo to paint the vault and the lunettes (1508-1512).*
The portrayal of the Day of Judgement on the altar wall was painted by Michelangelo by order of Pope Paul III between 1535 and 1541. It replaced frescos from the 15th century.
The restoration, now underway, has revealed Michelangelo's original colors in an unexpected, excellent vitality under the century-old layers of accumulated dust and smoke.

The "Biblioteca Apostolica Vaticana," called "la Vaticana" by scientists and researchers, contains about 70,000 manuscripts, 100,000 original texts, just as many prints and maps, a few thousand volumes of archives as well as a million printed books, including about 8,000 incunabula. It is the most famous library in the world. The Vaticana was first established as the pope's private library and was opened to scholars in the 15th century. The Vatican Library was officially opened on June 15, 1475. Pope Sixtus IV appointed Platina as the first librarian.

Recently, an international group of publishers and editors was formed to make the most valuable antique codices of the Vaticana available to scholars and the interested public as facsimile editions.

Opposite: *the Vaticana reading room.*

Above right: *Pope Alexander VI's Christmas missal, made between 1492 and 1503. The Christmas Mass begins on these richly decorated pages. Bottom: a medallion with Alexander VI's coat of arms and picture.*

Right: *Pope Nicholas V had manuscripts bought throughout Europe during his pontificate (1447-1455). Frescoes by Giovanni Battista Ricci in the "Sale Paoline" at the Vatican Library.*

The pope's private library is housed on the second floor of the Apostolic Palace. Rich in works of art from the Italian "trecento" and "quattrocento" periods, it also stores a collection of Bibles from different epochs and the writings of Church leaders in the cupboards on the walls, which date from the "cinquecento" period. The pope holds private audiences here with heads of state and ambassadors as well as cultural and political personalities.

Right: *The "Hall of the Savior" in the Apostolic Palace. The entrance to the pope's private chambers is located here.*

INDEX

MAP OF THE VATICAN

THE CONCLAVES
FROM 1276 TO 1978

THE POPES
FROM ST. PETER TO JOHN PAUL II.

Section of Raphael's "Transfiguration" in St. Peter's.

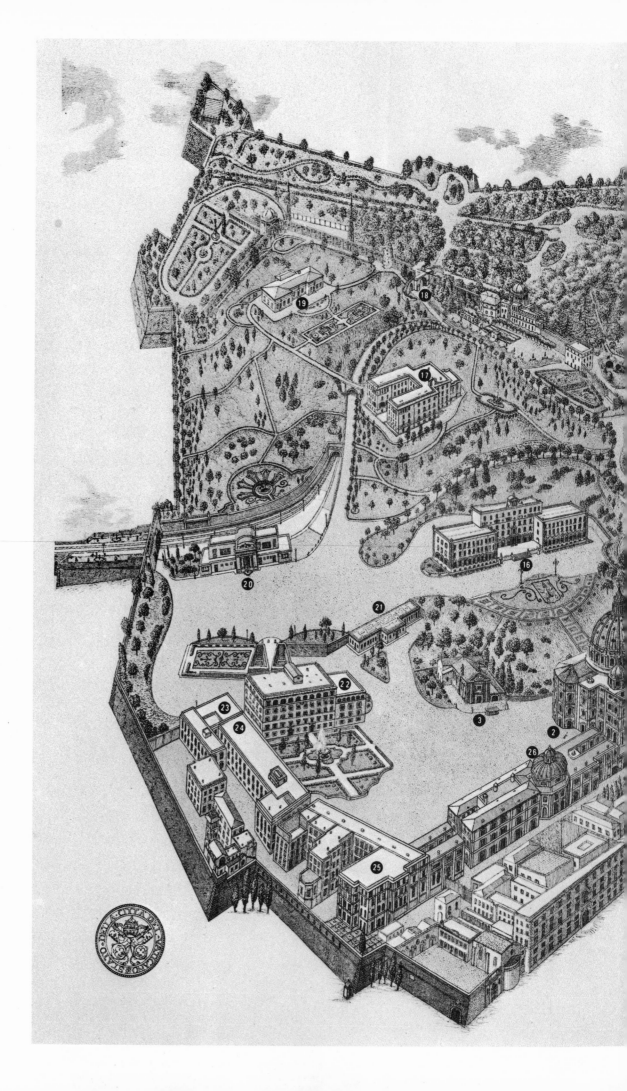

The Vatican

copperplate engraving
from the 19th century

1 – St. Peter's Square
2 – St. Peter's Basilica
3 – Chapel of St. Stephan
4 – Sistine Chapel
5 – Palace of S. Damaso
6 – Barracks of the Swiss Guards
7 – Church of St. Anna
8 – Vatican Printing Office
9 – Post Office
10 – Police
11 – Belvedere Palace
12 – Vatican Museums
13 – Loggias
14 – Vatican Library
15 – Art Gallery (Pinacoteca)
16 – Government Palace
17 – Ethiopian College
18 – Grotto of Lourdes
19 – Radio Vatican
20 – Railway Station
21 – School of Mosaics
22 – Court
23 – Residenza dell'Arciprete
24 – Palace of S. Carlo
25 – Hospice of St. Marta
26 – Canonica Sagrestia

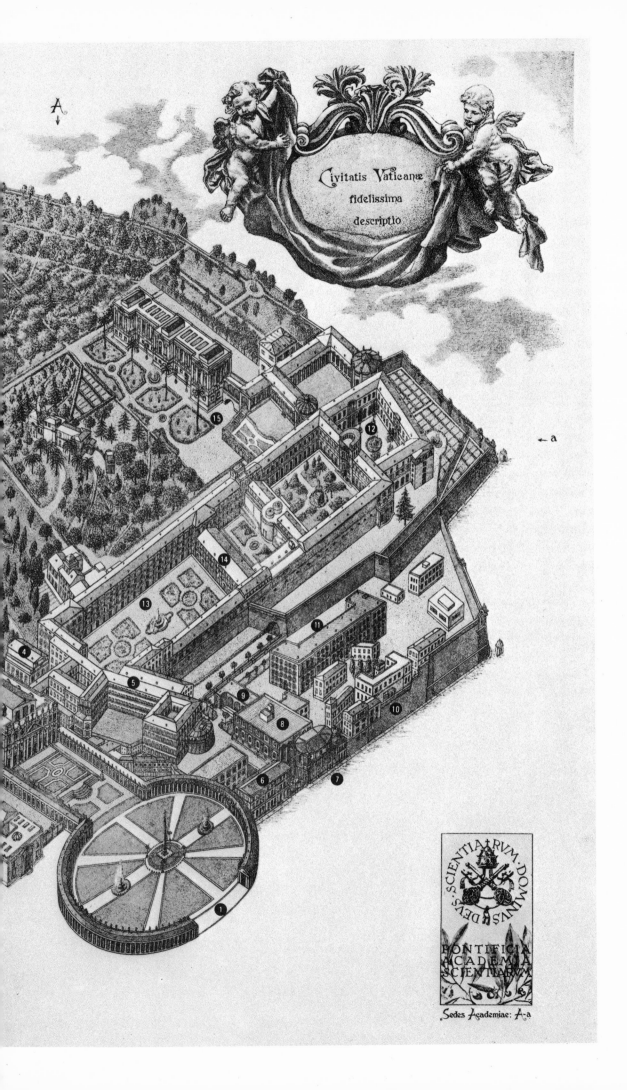

Civitatis Vaticanæ
fidelissima
descriptio

SCIENTIARVM·DOMINVS·DEVS·

PONTIFICIA
ACADEMIA
SCIENTIARVM

Sedes Academiae: A·a

The Conclaves
from 1276 to 1978

185. Blessed Innocent V	Arezzo 1276	1 day
186. Adrian V	Rome 1276	18 days
187. John XXI	Viterbo 1276	20 days
188. Nicholas III	Viterbo 1277	6 months
189. Martin IV	Viterbo 1280/81 (during the conclave, one cardinal died and two others were kidnapped)	6 months
190. Honorius	Perugia 1285	5 days
191. Nicholas IV	Rome 1288	1 year
192. St. Celestine V	Rome-Rieti-Anagni-Rome 1292—1294	2 years and 3 months
193. Boniface VIII	Naples 1294	1 day
194. Blessed Benedict XI	Perugia 1303	1 day
195. Clement V	Perugia 1305	11 months
196. John XXII	Carpentras 1314—1316	2 years and 3 months
197. Benedict XII	Avignon 1334	6 days
198. Clement VI	Avignon 1342	13 days
199. Innocent VI	Avignon 1352	12 days
200. Blessed Urban V	Avignon 1362	45 days
201. Gregory XI	Avignon 1370	1 day
202. Urban VI	Rome 1378	2 days
203. Boniface IX	Rome 1389	45 days
204. Innocent VII	Rome 1404	7 days
205. Gregory XII	Rome 1406	12 days
208. Martin V	Rome 1417	3 days
209. Eugene IV	Rome 1431	3 days
210. Nicholas V	Rome 1447	2 days
211. Calixtus III	Rome 1455	4 days
212. Pius II	Rome 1458	9 days
213. Paul II	Rome 1464	1 day
214. Sixtus IV	Rome 1471	3 days
215. Innocent VIII	Rome 1484	8 days
216. Alexander VI	Rome 1492	4 days
217. Pius III	Rome 1503	6 days
218. Julius II	Rome 1503	only a few hours
219. Leo X	Rome 1513	7 days
220. Adrian VI	Rome 1521/22	13 days
221. Clement VII	Rome 1523	50 days
222. Paul III	Rome 1534	2 days
223. Julius III	Rome 1549/50	70 days
224. Marcellus II	Rome 1555	6 days
225. Paul IV	Rome 1555	12 days
226. Pius IV	Rome 1559	4 months
227. St. Pius V	Rome 1565/66	17 days
228. Gregory XIII	Rome 1572	2 days
229. Sixtus V.	Rome 1585	4 days
230. Urban VII	Rome 1590	8 days
231. Gregory XIV	Rome 1590	60 days
232. Innocent IX	Rome 1591	1 day
233. Clement VIII	Rome 1592	20 days
234. Leo XI	Rome 1605	18 days
235. Paul V	Rome 1605	8 days
236. Gregory XV	Rome 1621	2 days
237. Urban VIII	Rome 1623	18 days
238. Innocent X	Rome 1644	46 days
239. Alexander VII	Rome 1655	50 days
240. Clement IX	Rome 1667	18 days
241. Clement X	Rome 1670	4 months
242. Blessed Innocent XI	Rome 1676	60 days
243. Alexander VIII	Rome 1689	51 days
244. Innocent XII	Rome 1691	5 months
245. Clement XI	Rome 1700	52 days
246. Innocent XIII	Rome 1721	30 days
247. Benedict XIII	Rome 1724	72 days
248. Clement XII	Rome 1730	over 4 months
249. Benedict XIV	Rome 1740	6 months
250. Clement XIII	Rome 1758	52 days
251. Clement XIV	Rome 1769	64 days
252. Pius VI	Rome 1775	over 4 months
253. Pius VII	Venice 1799—1800	3½ months
254. Leo XII	Rome 1823	26 days
255. Pius VIII	Rome 1829	somewhat longer than 1 month
256. Gregory XVI	Rome 1831	54 days
257. Pius IX	Rome 1846	somewhat longer than 2 days
258. Leo XIII	Rome 1878	1½ days
259. St. Pius X	Rome 1903	4 days
260. Benedict XV	Rome 1914	3 days
261. Pius XI	Rome 1922	4 days
262. Pius XII	Rome 1939	1 day
263. John XXIII	Rome 1958	3 days
264. Paul VI	Rome 1963	3 days
265. John Paul I	Rome August 1978	1 day
266. John Paul II	Rome October 1978	2 days

A portrayal of St. Liberius, pope from 352–366, from the 18th century. He was pope during the great Arian Schism and was banned to Thracia. According to legend, when he returned to Rome he marked out the foundations of the basilica of Santa Maria Maggiore during a snowstorm in August.

The Popes from St. Peter to John Paul II.

1.	St. Peter	† 64/67 (?)
2.	St. Linus	67—79 (?)
3.	St. Anacletus	79—90/92 (?)
4.	St. Clement I	90/92—101 (?)
5.	St. Evaristus	99/101—107 (?)
6.	St. Alexander I	107—116 (?)
7.	St. Sixtus I (Xystus)	116—125 (?)
8.	St. Telesphorus	125—138 (?)
9.	St. Hyginus	138—142 (?)
10.	St. Pius I	142—154/55 (?)
11.	St. Anicetus	154/155—166 (?)
12.	St. Soter	166—174 (?)
13.	St. Eleutherius	174—189 (?)
14.	St. Victor I	189—198/199 (?)
15.	St. Zephyrinus	199—217 (?)
16.	St. Calixtus I	217—222
	St. Hippolytus	217—235
17.	St. Urban I	222—230
18.	St. Pontianus	230—235
19.	St. Anterus	235—236
20.	St. Fabian	236—250
21.	St. Cornelius	251—253
	Novatian	251—258 (?)
22.	St. Lucius I	253—254
23.	St. Stephan I	254—257
24.	St. Sixtus II	257—258
25.	St. Dionysus	259/260—267/268
26.	St. Felix I	268/269—273/274
27.	St. Eutychianus	274/275—282/283
28.	St. Gaius	282/283—295/296
29.	St. Marcellinus	295/296—304
30.	St. Marcellus I	307—308 (?)
31.	St. Eusebius	308 [309/310]
32.	St. Miltiades (Melchiades)	310—314
33.	St. Silvester	314—335
34.	St. Marcus	336
35.	St. Julius I	337—352
36.	St. Liberius	352—366
	Felix II	355—358
37.	St. Damasus I	366—384
	Ursinus	366—367
38.	St. Siricius	384—399
39.	St. Anastasius I	399—402
40.	St. Innocent I	402—417
41.	St. Zosimus	417—419
	Eulalius	418—419
42.	St. Boniface I	419—422
43.	St. Celestine I	422—432
44.	St. Sixtus III	432—440
45.	St. Leo I	440—461
46.	St. Hilarius	461—468
47.	St. Simplicius	468—483
48.	St. Felix II (III)	483—492
49.	St. Gelasius I	492—496
50.	Anastasius II	496—498
51.	St. Symmachus	498—514
	Laurentius	498—506
52.	St. Hormisdas	514—523
53.	St. John I	523—526
54.	St. Felix III (IV)	526—530
55.	Boniface II	530—532
	Dioscorus	530
56.	John II (Mercurius)	533—535
57.	St. Agapetus I	535—536
58.	St. Silverius	536—537
59.	Vigilius	537—555
60.	Pelagius I	556—561
61.	John III	561—574
62.	Benedict I	575—579
63.	Pelagius II	579—590
64.	St. Gregory I	590—604
65.	Sabinian	604—606
66.	Boniface III	607
67.	St. Boniface IV	608—615
68.	St. Deusdedit (Adeodatus I)	615—618
69.	Boniface V	619—625
70.	Honorius I	625—638
71.	Severinus	640
72.	John IV	640—643
73.	Theodore I	643—649
74.	St. Martin I	649—653
75.	St. Eugenius I	654—657
76.	St. Vitalianus	657—672
77.	Adeodatus II	672—676
78.	Donus	676—678
79.	St. Agatho	678—681
80.	St. Leo II	682—683
81.	St. Benedict II	684—685
82.	John V	685—686
83.	Conon	686—687
	Theodore	687
	Pashal	687
84.	St. Sergius I	687—701
85.	John VI	701—705
86.	John VII	705—707
87.	Sisinnius	708
88.	Constantine I	708—715
89.	St. Gregory II	715—731
90.	St. Gregory III	731—741
91.	St. Zacharias	741—752
	Stephen II	752
92.	Stephen II (III)	752—757
93.	St. Paul I	757—767
	Constantine II	767—768
	Philip	768
94.	Stephen III (IV)	768—772
95.	Adrian I	772—795
96.	St. Leo III	795—816
97.	Stephen IV (V)	816—817
98.	St. Pashal I	817—824
99.	Eugenius II	824—827
100.	Valentinus	827
101.	Gregory IV	827—844
	John	844
102.	Sergius II	844—847
103.	St. Leo IV	847—855
104.	Benedict III	855—858
	Anastasius III	855
105.	St. Nicholas I	858—867
106.	Adrian II	867—872
107.	John VIII	872—882
108.	Marinus I (Martin II)	882—884
109.	St. Adrian III	884—885
110.	Stephen V (VI)	885—891
111.	Formosus	891—896
112.	Boniface VI	896
113.	Stephen VI (VII)	896—897
114.	Romanus	897
115.	Theodore II	897
116.	John IX	898—900
117.	Benedict IV	900—903
118.	Leo V	903
119.	Christopher	903—904

#	Pope	Reign
120.	Sergius III	904—911
121.	Anastasius III	911—913
122.	Lando	913—914
123.	John X	914—928
124.	Leo VI	928
125.	Stephen VII (VIII)	929—931
126.	John XI	931—935
127.	Leo VII	936—939
128.	Stephen VIII (IX)	939—942
129.	Marinus II (Martin III)	942—946
130.	Agapetus II	946—955
131.	John XII	955—963
132.	Leo VIII	963—965
133.	Benedict V	964
134.	John XIII	965—972
135.	Benedict VI	973—974
	Boniface VII (Franco)	974
136.	Benedict VII	974—983
137.	John XIV	983—984
138.	Boniface VII	984—985
139.	John XV	985—996
140.	Gregory V	996—999
	John XVI	997—998
141.	Silvester II	999—1003
142.	John XVII	1003
143.	John XVIII	1003/04—1009
144.	Sergius IV	1009—1012
145.	Benedict VIII	1012—1024
	Gregory VI	1012
146.	John XIX	1024—1032
147.	Benedict IX	1032—1045
	Silvester III	1045
148.	Gregory VI	1045—1046
149.	Clement II	1046—1047
150.	Damasus II	1048
151.	St. Leo IX	1049—1054
152.	Victor II	1055—1057
153.	Stephen IX (X)	1057—1058
154.	Benedict X	1058—1059
155.	Nicholas II	1059—1061
156.	Alexander II	1061—1073
	Honorius II	1061—1071/72
157.	St. Gregory VII	1073—1085
	Clement III	1080—1100
158.	Blessed Victor III	1086—1087
159.	Blessed Urban II	1088—1099
160.	Pashal II	1099—1118
	Theodoric	1100—1102
	Albert	1102
	Silvester IV	1105—1111
161.	Gelasius II	1118—1119
	Gregory VIII	1118—1121
162.	Calixtus II	1119—1124
163.	Honorius II	1124—1130
	Celestine II	1124
164.	Innocent II	1130—1143
	Anacletus II	1130—1138
	Victor IV	1138
165.	Celestine II	1143—1144
166.	Lucius II	1144—1145
167.	Blessed Eugenius III	1145—1153
168.	Anastasius IV	1153—1154
169.	Adrian IV	1154—1159
170.	Alexander III	1159—1181
	Victor IV	1159—1164
	Pashal III	1164—1168
	Calixtus III	1168—1178
	Innocent III	1179—1180
171.	Lucius III	1181—1185
172.	Urban III	1185—1187
173.	Gregory VIII	1187
174.	Clement III	1187—1191
175.	Celestine III	1191—1198
176.	Innocent III	1198—1216
177.	Honorius III	1216—1227
178.	Gregory IX	1227—1241
179.	Celestine IV	1241
180.	Innocent IV	1243—1254
181.	Alexander IV	1254—1261
182.	Urban IV	1261—1264
183.	Clement IV	1265—1268
184.	Blessed Gregory X	1271—1276
185.	Blessed Innocent V	1276
186.	Adrian V	1276
187.	John XXI	1276—1277
188.	Nicholas III	1277—1280
189.	Martin IV	1281—1285
190.	Honorius IV	1285—1287
191.	Nicholas IV	1288—1292
192.	St. Celestine V	1294
193.	Boniface VIII	1294—1303
194.	Blessed Benedict XI	1303—1304
195.	Clement V	1305—1314
196.	John XXII	1316—1334
	Nicholas V	1328—1330
197.	Benedict XII	1334—1342
198.	Clement VI	1342—1352
199.	Innocent VI	1352—1362
200.	Blessed Urban V	1362—1370
210.	Gregory XI	1370—1378
202.	Urban VI	1378—1389
	Clement VII	1378—1394
203.	Boniface IX	1389—1404
	Benedict XIII	1394—1423
204.	Innocent VII	1404—1406
205.	Gregory XII	1406—1415
206.	Alexander V	1409—1410
207.	John XXIII	1410—1415
208.	Martin V	1417—1431
	Clement VIII	1423—1429
209.	Eugenius IV	1431—1447
	Felix V	1439—1449
210.	Nicholas V	1447—1455
211.	Calixtus III	1455—1458
212.	Pius II	1458—1464
213.	Paul II	1464—1471
214.	Sixtus IV	1471—1484
215.	Innocent VIII	1484—1492
216.	Alexander VI	1492—1503
217.	Pius III	1503
218.	Julius II	1503—1513
219.	Leo X	1513—1521
220.	Adrian VI	1522—1523
221.	Clement VII	1523—1534
222.	Paul III	1534—1549
223.	Julius III	1550—1555
224.	Marcellus II	1555
225.	Paul IV	1555—1559
226.	Pius IV	1559—1565
227.	St. Pius V	1566—1572
228.	Gregory XIII	1572—1585
229.	Sixtus V	1585—1590
230.	Urban VII	1590
231.	Gregory XIV	1590—1591
232.	Innocent IX	1591
233.	Clement VIII	1592—1605
234.	Leo XI	1605
235.	Paul V	1605—1621
236.	Gregory XV	1621—1623
237.	Urban VIII	1623—1644
238.	Innocent X	1644—1655

239. Alexander VII	1655—1667
240. Clement IX	1667—1669
241. Clement X	1670—1676
242. Blessed Innocent XI	1676—1689
243. Alexander VIII	1689—1691
244. Innocent XII	1691—1700
245. Clement XI	1700—1721
246. Innocent XIII	1721—1724
247. Benedict XIII	1724—1730
248. Clement XII	1730—1740
249. Benedict XIV	1740—1758
250. Clement XIII	1758—1769
251. Clement XIV	1769—1774
252. Pius VI	1775—1799
253. Pius VII	1800—1823
254. Leo XII	1823—1829
255. Pius VIII	1829—1830
256. Gregory XVI	1831—1846
257. Pius IX	1846—1878
258. Leo XIII	1878—1903
259. St. Pius X	1903—1914
260. Benedict XV	1914—1922
261. Pius XI	1922—1939
262. Pius XII	1939—1958
263. John XXIII	1958—1963
264. Paul VI	1963—1978
265. John Paul I	1978
266. John Paul II	since 1978

Pope Pius VII being carried through the basilica on a sedan. The two large "flabella" (fans made of white peacock feathers) are no longer used today. The sedan was last put to use during the Mass celebrated by Pope Paul VI in St. John Lateran for Aldo Moro, a statesman killed by members of the Red Brigades.